THE VOICE OF LATIN AMERICA

HARPER & BROTHERS, NEW YORK

THE VOICE OF LATIN AMERICA

WILLIAM BENTON

THE VOICE OF LATIN AMERICA

PRINTED IN THE UNITED STATES OF AMERICA

FIRST EDITION

LIBRARY OF CONGRESS CATALOG CARD NUMBER: 61-12227

CONTENTS

FOREWORD

by Adlai E. Stevenson

A great deal of what North Americans think they know about Central and South America isn't so. And a very great deal of what they don't know about Central and South America is both important and fascinating.

Here is a book that proves once again that truth can be more interesting than the folklore it displaces.

I write these words in the late Spring of 1961. Over recent months Latin-American affairs have drawn more attention from the U.S. press and public than at any time in our century. When it is suddenly increased, such attention can add to the inherited burden of misunderstanding; it can deepen the stereotypes and aggravate the clichés. But the people of the Americas can't afford the luxury of clichés and stereotypes any longer. This new burst of mutual interest must become a first long stride toward the day when English-speaking, Spanish-speaking, and Portuguese-speaking Americans (and French-speaking, too) will know each other as they are.

This book by my friend William Benton will be extraordinarily useful in promoting such mutual hemispheric acquaintance—and on a plane of candor. It is a book which will be timely for years to come. Its analyses will survive the gusts of incident. It will be read and re-read because Latin America is destined for developments that will affect the well-being of the entire world for as long as we can foresee.

Because better understanding (and, conversely, the amputation of reasons for distrust) among the American peoples is imperative, I commend this report to every literate citizen. I hope the text will soon be available in several languages. No single set of steps Latin Americans take on the world scene without us, nor any programs we undertake without them, can be as meaningful as the work we do in concert.

Bill Benton and I journeyed together on an engrossing trip. His report reflects much of what we heard and saw. There is already in print excellent survey material on what U.S.-Latin American policies have been, are, and should be. Nowhere I know of, however, has there been such a well-disciplined selection of what is important, fresher observation, or such lively and succinct discussion about what the American peoples can do in partnership.

I have known Bill Benton for three decades. He has that versatility of mind and interest we associate with the Renaissance and with our American founders. The Honorable William Benton has so many active interests and successful careers that he is, appropriately, the Chairman of the Board of an encyclopaedia (I know of nothing which does not interest him!). He appears comfortably at home in the realms of education, publishing, business, scholarly and popular writing on an astonishing range of topics, government, philanthropy, politics, and the arts.

Thus he brings a whole repertory of seasoned competences to bear on any task he takes on. Here he deals with authority on several key questions—economic development, political tension and torsion, educational logistics, mass communication needs, to mention a few.

Especially impressive here are his appraisals of why there is a pervasive heritage of anti-Yanqui attitudes throughout Latin America; why economic and educational requirements there are so formidable; and how difficult it will be for even the ablest new political leaders—and there are many—to reconcile responsible policies with the ability to remain in office.

Both of us derived bright, lasting pleasures from the fine men and women we met, and from whom we learned much. Time and again I have heard Benton mention the right historic reference in the particular country we were in. Encountering a creative, social, artistic, or archeological masterpiece, his excitement is invariably spontaneous and eloquent. And that makes what is best of all—a good traveling companion.

I concur with what he has written about the decisions our Latin friends must make for themselves. And I share his confident expectation that the United States will prove itself in future to be a far more effective supporter of Latin American aspirations than it has been in the past. President Kennedy set forth these factors plainly in his incisive address at his first White House reception for Latin American diplomats when he said:

Only the determined efforts of the American nations themselves can bring success to this effort (speaking of the new "alianza para progreso"). *They, and they alone, can mobilize their resources—enlist the energies of their people—and modify their social patterns so that all, and not just a privileged few, share in the fruits of growth. If this effort is made, then outside assistance will give a vital impetus to progress. Without it, no amount of help will advance the welfare of the people.*

The level of understanding we seek won't be reached quickly, and certainly not merely by yearning that it come to pass, since understanding requires a resonance of signals, with both parties sending and receiving intelligible messages. We cannot delay decisions until the new plateau is reached. Such understanding will best come when the American peoples work constructively together on tangible, mutually useful undertakings.

This book tells of some notably promising beginnings. Let us carry these starts forward, multiplying the application of lessons as they are learned.

A PERSONAL PREFACE

This book is stimulated by a trip taken by Governor Stevenson and me through Latin America in the spring of 1960. Until then —the year both of us reached 60—neither of us had ever been in the great cities of South America. Like so many of our nomadic fellow citizens we had journeyed to Mexico City and Havana—but not to the capitals of the new world's southern hemisphere. However, the problems of Latin America were not unknown to us. In my own case, I had dealt with Latin American matters at earlier times and places—as a special consultant to Nelson Rockefeller before and during World War II after he took office as Co-ordinator of Inter-American Affairs; as a U.S. delegate to eight official international conferences, two of which were held in Mexico City and one other of which was devoted to inter-American development; as Assistant Secretary of State, in which post I inherited many of Nelson Rockefeller's hemispheric responsibilities, and as U.S. Senator.

It is one thing to deal with the affairs of a country or region as they appear in governmental documents or in conferences. It is quite a different thing to absorb the temper of a people by being physically among them—and particularly, to absorb it in the setting of their capital cities. This, Governor Stevenson had been able to do in Africa and Asia during the previous seven years when he crisscrossed much of both continents. I had been able to do so in Asia not long before the war, when I had spent much of a year there. Above all, Governor Stevenson and I had been able to do this in Europe over the preceding 30 years during which each of us had crossed the Atlantic times without number.

Our concentration on the old world is easy to understand. But is the relative neglect of travel to Latin America—shared with us by so many residents of the United States—is this a symptom of widespread U.S. indifference, as many Latin Americans believe? I rather think that it is. We North Americans have been indifferent to teaching about Latin America in our schools. In our universities we have neglected Latin America as a field for scholarship. In our diplomacy we have failed to encourage adequately the legitimate political aspirations of our neighbors to the south. And in our foreign economic policy we have given nearly exclusive emphasis to Europe and Asia: only about 2% of our foreign economic aid since World War II had gone to Latin America. This is now being changed. President Kennedy, in his plan for the Americas, has called for ten years "of maximum effort—the years when the greatest obstacles must be overcome—the years when the need for assistance will be the greatest."

Perhaps our long-standing underemphasis on Latin America grew from a false sense of geographical security. On the map, the countries south of the Rio Grande appear as the area of the world least menaced by a Soviet or Chinese military threat (even through Cuba!). But if this is true—and it probably is—the implication may be the reverse. These are the countries geographically closest to us on which, in time of crisis, we are most dependent. Even in the narrow military sense, the oil and bauxite and copper of Latin America are indispensable to the defense of the hemisphere and thus of the free world. More importantly, Latin America will increasingly prove to be one of the great battlegrounds in the nonmilitary struggle between our system and the Communist system—a struggle which seems sure to dominate the rest of the 20th century. The Latin republics may now appear more resistant to the Communist ideology than some other underdeveloped areas of the earth. But nothing I saw there made me complacent. Many think they are softening, and I among them. During the next decade and thereafter the fight against Communism in and by Latin America may turn out to be as important to the U. S. and to the free world as that in any other part of the globe.

Those who feel that the Communist drive against the U.S.A. is weakening should expose themselves to the new Communist "manifesto"—a statement which Communist leaders of 81 countries issued in concert following a party congress in Moscow, November, 1960—and to Khrushchev's address to the Party organizations of the Soviet Union a month later in January. In both these statements the Communists, much as Hitler did in his *Mein Kampf*, set forth in precise and confident detail their objectives and plans for world domination.

Charles Burton Marshall warned us that, whether or not we assume as valid the attribution of a lesser degree of militancy to the Soviet Union than to Red China, "the important question is how militant does the Soviet Union remain? Khrushchev's speech gives us an answer. The Soviet intention is to do us in—thoroughly, finally and explicitly."

Both the new manifesto and Khrushchev's speech about it assert the triumph of world communism within a calculable future. The manifesto, in theory at least, accepts the Khrushchev doctrine that the Communist states are powerful enough to win the world without war, but it makes entirely clear that the Communist world would and should resort to war where this is necessary to achieve Communist aims. And Khrushchev himself defines the policy of peaceful coexistence as "a form of intense, economic, political, and ideological struggle between the proletariat and the aggressive forces of imperialism in the world arena."

In both documents the United States is designated as the chief obstacles in the path of Communist world domination. The United States is the "chief imperialist country of today," the "biggest international exploiter," "the chief bulwark of world reaction and an international gendarme," and an "enemy of the peoples of the whole world." This obsession with the United States as the supreme enemy is perhaps the most ominous aspect of these documents.

With reference to Latin America one statement asserts that "more than any other capitalist country, the United States drains Asia, and especially Latin America of their riches, holding up their progress." Further and more importantly, it reports that a "front of active struggle against imperialism has opened in Latin America." Khrushchev himself declares that while formerly "Latin America was bound hand and foot to Yankee imperialism. . . . Today, the Latin American peoples are showing by their struggle that the American continent is not a manorial estate of the U.S.A. Latin America is reminiscent of an active volcano. . . . Solidarity with revolutionary Cuba is the duty not only of the Latin American peoples, but also of the Socialist countries, the entire international Communist movement and the proletariat all over the world."

Thus belatedly in 1960, Governor Stevenson and I devoted intensive months to 12 Latin-American countries. Counterclockwise facing south, we flew to Mexico, Guatemala, Costa Rica, Panama, Colombia, Ecuador, Peru, Chile, Argentina, Uruguay, Brazil and Venezuela. We talked with 11 of the 12 presidents of these countries, and with the prime minister of Peru whose president was in Europe. We met with cabinet ministers, with leaders of the opposition, with intellectuals, labor leaders and students.

I must here pronounce a warning. I am of course pleased that Governor Stevenson in his foreword states that he believes that this report of mine "will be timely for years to come." Nevertheless I should point out that my interviews in Latin America took place before the U.S. presidential election of 1960; before President Kennedy's "Alliance for Progress" proposals and the action of Congress in voting half a billion dollars to support them; before the unhappy landing of anti-Castro refugees at the Bay of Pigs; and before the assassination of Trujillo. I do not believe these events materially change my basic analysis—indeed, perhaps they emphasize it—but the *caveat* must be made.

I would not recommend to the tourist seeking a good time the regime to which the Governor and I were subjected. Always our schedule of 16-hour days was unusual. Our Latin-American hosts and the U.S. embassies vied with each other in homicidal hospitality. Often this meant ceremony and protocol: the 2½- or 3-hour luncheon with its emphasis on speeches rather than informal give and take with a few key people; the late dinner and reception with toasts and speeches and brandy still being served at 1 A.M., six hours before plane time. When we wanted to visit the rector of a university and a few of his professors, often we arrived to find a couple of hundred professors with students and a schedule of speeches. All of this was complimentary and much of it was instructive, but it was not the best way to relax—nor was it always the best way to learn the facts of political life.

The first day of our journey—in Mexico City—was not untypical. The city is 7,500 feet high and my doctor had warned me we should allow a full day to adjust ourselves to the altitude. Our tourist plane from Chicago arrived at night an hour or more late. Dinnerless, we got to the hotel about 10:30 to find the Overseas Press club waiting for us in their new clubrooms. We met with them until about 1 o'clock, gulping scrambled eggs and Coca-Cola.

The next morning we were up at 7. At 9:30 our able and hardworking ambassador, Robert C. Hill of New Hampshire, had the entire staff of the embassy to greet us in the embassy's gardens —about five or six hundred people. We gave little speeches. I spoke of the fact that I had first seen this lovely garden in 1935 at Ambassador Josephus Daniels' Fourth of July party for the visiting schoolteachers. I spoke of my many exposures to the garden when I was a delegate at the Inter-American Conference on Problems of War and Peace in 1945 (the so-called Chapultepec conference) and later in 1947 when I spent six weeks in Mexico City as chairman of the U.S. delegation of the second UNESCO conference.

Then we had our "briefing" by Ambassador Hill and his embassy officials—until some time around noon when we called on

Foreign Minister Manuel Tello. This visit was followed by his three-hour formal luncheon of welcome, and this in turn by a visit to the Palacio de Bellas Artes with the famous Mexican artist Rufino Tamayo, to see his murals. Back at the hotel at 5:05, with no time for a siesta, we were picked up at 5:40 for a call at 6 on Pres. Adolfo Lopez Mateos. From the president's mansion we were rushed to the U.S. Embassy at 7:30 to stand in line to shake hands with 750 people. We were still on our feet after 10 o'clock —and with no supper—but with a well-pleased ambassador and staff.

Throughout the trip, Governor Stevenson was infinitely patient. The entire two-month-long journey was a great personal triumph for him. He seems known to almost every Latin American. He was besieged everywhere by admiring crowds seeking autographs, bows, handshakes and smiles. Though we traveled strictly as private citizens, his appearances became a triumph also for the United States; he symbolizes, in his learning, his wisdom and wit, his urbanity, oratory and his humane qualities, the characteristics the Latin Americans most value in their intellectuals and political leaders. (This is of course why President Kennedy asked him to revisit Latin America, to duplicate our trip though in condensed and capsule form, as his representative in June of '61.)

The following report is neither a journal nor a travelogue. It leaves out much but seeks to emphasize some general impressions and key conclusions. It makes no pretense of being complete or definitive in any way.

Whatever value it may have will flow not from its "expert" character, or its scholarship, but from the fact that as earnest and experienced learners we asked many of the right questions— and we were usually talking to men who wanted to give us the right answers.

We did of course see some of the "sights," though I am not elaborating upon them. The sights everyone should try to see include not only such natural wonders as the Andes but the breath-taking Mayan and Incan archaeological sites in Yucatan and Peru. For fishermen, a paradise awaits in the rushing streams and beautiful lakes of volcano-studded southern Chile. Quickly we began to appreciate how vast and varied is Latin America. We saw modern buildings rising at a feverish rate in Mexico City, in Sao Paulo, Brasilia and elsewhere—buildings that for brilliant architecture and imaginative use of local materials have no counterpart in the United States. In Lima, Rio de Janeiro and most of the big cities we also saw festering slums in the very shadows of tall luxurious apartment houses—slums where as much as 20% of the city's population exists in unbelievable squalor. We dined in presidential palaces adorned by tapestries, serenaded by bands and surrounded by magnificently gold-encrusted trappings from the 19th century. And we ate hamburgers with university students in the Tunjuelito of Bogota. We visited great ranches in Brazil and Argentina on which millions of tons of meat—kept out of U.S. markets because of foot-and-mouth disease—are produced for Europe. We saw thousands of sleek, expensive automobiles in oil-rich Caracas and barefoot Indians pulling wooden plows in the fields of Peru—where the per capita income is only $100 per year.

But most of all we listened. And at the end of each day I dictated into a machine—about 160,000 words in all—or enough to fill a couple of full-length books. Upon these daily memorandums, this book is largely based.

One hundred travelers to Latin America would write one hundred different reports. The perspective I carried with me, out of my own personal background, gives this report its theme. I am deeply concerned about the future foreign policy of the United States and about the policy of the free world. What are the central problems, the key facts, the emergent trends in Latin America which bear on these policies? Can the United States and the free world—through better understanding of these problems, facts, and trends—develop policies better designed to advance the freedom, the progress, and the security of all?

In this perspective of mine, three great Latin-American problems now seem paramount—the lack of economic development, the threat of Communism, and the paucity of education. Each of these three is given a major section in this report.

The current world struggle, plus the immense variety of Latin America and its rapidity of change, now force upon Latin America and North America alike the necessity for a better understanding of our common goals. We are, at long last, beginning to plan for the future in terms of those goals. It is a far wiser course than taking historical potluck as we had largely been doing.

It would be false to say that I felt encouraged at the end of the trip. Yes, we had met gifted and indeed heroic men along the way. The social projects they had begun were visible on all sides. Nevertheless, when I said my good-bys, it was with a foreboding fear that the start of better things to come might be despoiled in the not far distant future. Whether or not this happens will depend in large part on the quality of hemispheric leadership—and not least in this balance will be the skill and courage of the leadership of the United States. This fact should be kept in mind by the reader as he peruses this report. Our Presidents for decades to come will need the support and informed judgments of concerned citizens.

My personal recommendations for U.S. policy are given in the closing section.

Many men who know Latin America far better than I have helped inform and educate me—and none more than Carleton Sprague Smith, head of the Brazilian Institute of New York University. Dr. Smith accompanied Governor Stevenson and me throughout the trip as guide, friend, interpreter and mentor.

Dr. Kenneth Holland assembled an outstanding group at his Institute of International Education to brief us before we left, and Professor Kalman Silvert of Tulane University wrote special country-by-country memorandums for us which became my main airplane reading. On the journey itself, government officials —many of whom are here quoted—and U.S. embassy staffs were unfailingly cordial and cooperative; among the latter, Albion

Patterson of our embassy in Buenos Aires, a dedicated civil servant, was notably helpful. Parts or all of the manuscript were read by Professors Frank Tannenbaum and Harold Clark of Columbia University; Serafino Romualdi of the AFL-CIO; Professor Harold Benjamin of George Peabody College; and Edward Miller, Jr., former U.S. Assistant Secretary of State for Inter-American Affairs. I am grateful to all of them and I absolve them of responsibility. Finally, I am indebted for most careful editing to Robert W. Murphey, managing editor of the *Encyclopaedia Britannica Book of the Year*, in whose 1961 edition the major part of this material appeared for the first time.

William Benton

Southport, Connecticut

1

The Voice of Latin America Has Many Accents

An Introduction

Is there such an entity as "Latin America"? If there is, and I think there is, can it be said, even rhetorically, to have a voice? Many of the experienced men who helped brief us before our trip warned that the great amorphous region called Latin America comprises 20 highly individualistic independent nations. These countries do not speak with a single voice. They have voices which make up a chorus, often harmonious but sometimes discordant. To think of them as a unit—or to treat them as if they were a single nation or a single people—invites grave misunderstanding and confusion.

But these 20 republics have more in common than a joint tenancy of their quarter of the globe. They share a common background of Iberian culture, a common religion and the frontier freshness that is still the mark of the Americas. (Frank Tannenbaum, one of the foremost U.S. scholars in the field of Latin-American studies, is struck by the similarity in the outlook of their intellectuals—especially when they think of the United States!)

And of course they share common problems. In varying degrees almost all are plagued with poverty, illiteracy, hunger, ill-health, inflation, political corruption and economic backwardness. In most of them, population is growing at a rate even higher than that of some of the old champions of the orient. The economies of most depend on exports of one or two commodities. In some measure, all retain the characteristics of a feudal society; even though a middle class is developing, the chasm between rich and poor often seems to be getting wider rather than narrower.

Restlessness and discontent are characteristic. Foreign Minister Tello of Mexico warned us on our first stop that all the peoples of Latin America could be described with just one word—"impatient."

Geographically, Latin America is cut off from the rest of the world by vast oceans; internally its parts are almost equally isolated. Throughout their colonial and national histories, the 20 countries have had more intimate communications with Europe and the United States than with each other. The west coast is blocked off from the rest of the continent by the Andes range that runs south 4,400 mi. from Venezuela to the tip of Chile. Its mountain passes are few, narrow and in many cases three miles high. They have been scarcely usable as commercial routes. Gen. José de San Martín's feat in 1817 of crossing the Andes from the Argentine into Chile with a small army is a military exploit that ranks with Hannibal's crossing the Alps.

Along the east coast of the continent another range extends about 1,700 mi. To the north is the Amazon basin, where very heavy rains, dense forests and leached soils have prevented settlement by Europeans. There, in an area of 2,700,000 sq. mi., the population is less than one person per square mile.

Somewhat more than 25% of South America is mountainous. Close to 25% is very swampy; 10% or more is desert or extremely dry.

The vast majority of Latin America's peoples, as a result of its geography, live within 200 mi. of the coasts. Most of the biggest cities—Rio de Janeiro, Buenos Aires, São Paulo, Lima, Caracas,

Montevideo, Santiago and Valparaíso—lie on or near the Atlantic or Pacific oceans. Exceptions are Bogotá and Mexico City. Unlike many urban centres of the United States, where the suburban areas are often more populous than the cities at their cores, the cities of Latin America end abruptly at the outskirts.

Rural Latin Americans have for centuries bunched themselves in small towns and villages where they live within themselves, shut off from the rest of the world. Ninety-nine per cent of the place names refer to settlements with fewer than 2,000 inhabitants who are largely illiterate and where word from the outside world filters in slowly. Yet Montevideo contains more than half of Uruguay's population and greater Buenos Aires houses almost one third of Argentina's.

The provincialism of physical isolation expresses itself in attitudes of mixed pride and mistrust. Even in the cities the mutual interdependence springing from interlocking occupations has not served to override the sense of suspicion. Further, within each country there is distrust of the 19 others.

Pervading all is distrust of "Yanqui imperialism" and "big business," British and European as well as American. The distrust is so deep, widespread and of such long standing that it must be reckoned with in nearly every inter-American problem confronting the U.S. today. Thus it occupies a key role in this report.

The Three Latin Americas—Divided by Race

Common usage defines three Latin Americas: Indian Latin America, European Latin America and Mestizo Latin America.

INDIAN populations of relatively "high culture" (in the ethnological sense) live pretty much where the Spaniards encountered them in the early 16th century during the conquest. Indian Latin America includes high mountain areas from the U.S. border south to Paraguay. In dense concentration Indians are found from the waist of the Isthmus of Tehuantepec in Mexico, and the thumb of Yucatán south through Guatemala. They taper off through the remainder of Central America to dwindle away at the northern border of Costa Rica. Their density picks up once more in parts of Colombia, grows very heavy in Ecuador, and by the millions they cover the Andean ridge through Peru and Bolivia. Thus Indian Latin America includes large parts of Mexico, Guatemala, Ecuador, Peru and Bolivia; in other countries they lack sufficient numbers to affect significantly the tone of the evolving national cultures. Their total numbers range from 14,000,000 to 30,000,000, depending on the definition of an Indian—that is, between 1 in 14 and 1 in 6 of Latin America's 198,000,000 people.

EUROPEAN LATIN AMERICA, the second Latin America, is commonly thought of as including Argentina, Uruguay, Chile and Costa Rica. The first washes of migration from Europe brought the Spaniards and Portuguese. Later mass migrations brought many Italians, especially to Argentina and Uruguay; plus Germans, whose cultural influence is strongly felt in Chile and in parts of Argentina and Brazil; plus other central and eastern European stocks. Light sprinklings of Chinese, Japanese and Levantines are also found in many Latin-American countries.

THE MESTIZOS comprise the third group. A Mestizo is a mixture of European and Indian. Usually the word refers to the actual racial mixture, the physical mingling of "blood." Sometimes, however, it is sufficient that an Indian be of European or Mestizo culture for him to be accepted as Mestizo. Ecuador's former Pres. Galo Plaza told me the common saying that an Indian stops being an Indian when he takes off his poncho.

Mestizo Latin America comprises a major part of Mexico, El Salvador, Honduras, Nicaragua, Panamá, Colombia, Venezuela, Paraguay and the Dominican Republic. Haiti, peopled by the descendants of African slaves and speaking a patois of French, is a special case. Brazil too must be judged separately. Because of its huge size (one third of Latin America's population and an area greater than that of conterminous United States) and its special population mixture (Portuguese, Dutch, Indian, Italian, Japanese, German and almost 40% Negro and brown races), Brazil is a world unto itself, its own kind of "Mestizo Brazilian America."

The early aristocratic colonial governments, which reserved

the topmost administrative jobs for those sent from Spain (the *peninsulares*), with occasional generosity toward the child of Spanish parents born in the new world (the *criollo*), treated the Mestizo as an inferior. Strong currents of this prejudice still exist in certain countries, although the events of the century and a half since independence from Spain and Portugal have served as a powerful stimulus to the elevation of the mestizo. In many countries, the turbulence and civil wars of the 19th century resulted in the destruction of the monopolistic social power of the leading families. This gave the Mestizo his opportunity. It permitted him to become the dominant ethnic influence in such countries as Mexico and Venezuela. Everywhere, he has become the master of the Indian. He has risen to important military and political positions, adopting many of the ways of his European mentors and marrying into the families of aristocratic tradition. Driven by his determination to achieve status and power, the Mestizo in those lands where his numbers are great has taken over leadership. Everywhere except in the most European of the countries, today's presidents, cabinet members, industrialists and university professors are likely to be Mestizos.

THE NEGRO is the fourth racial group, along with the Indians, Europeans and Mestizos, that plays a part in the complicated heritage of Latin America. During the colonial period Negroes were brought in greater or lesser numbers to every country from Cuba to Chile, although there are today few Negroes in the populous countries of Chile and Argentina. However, in Brazil, which contains the greatest concentration, and throughout much of Latin America the Negro is not handicapped by the same type of color prejudice found in the United States.

Señora Virginia Pérez, the attractive and only daughter of Pres. Rómulo Betancourt of Venezuela, while she was escorting us through the slums of Caracas, told us her mother's term of affection for her father is *negro* (which is Spanish for "black" or "dark"), his for her mother is *negra* and that of both parents for her is *negrita*. Thus the feeling towards dark-skinned persons is sufficiently relaxed to permit the use of such words as terms of endearment—although to us they carry a racial connotation.

Prejudice does exist in Latin America, and often is deeply embedded, but it is not based on the feeling that people of color are inferior. In most countries, any Negro or Indian who can escape from his poverty and who can acquire an education and the ways and dress of the European and Mestizo may find an opportunity to attain wealth and political power. In many countries of Latin America the division between upper and lower classes is far more marked than in the United States. This division is in the aristocratic class tradition. The decisive factors are wealth and power, not race or color.

The Three Latin Americas—by Temperament and Outlook

The population of the Latin-American republics can be divided in another and most useful way. This is in terms of how various groups act and react—and what they may do and hope for. I suggest three main categories: The Vocifereous Ones, The Resisters and The Silent Ones (who may not remain silent much longer).

THE VOCIFEROUS ONES speak with the loudest voice. They make the headlines. They expel traditional dictators, build new industries, reform governments and often maladminister them. In politics they may be conservative, leftist or centrist, but most of them accept democracy as the political ideal most consonant with human dignity. The new cities and industries mothered them; western political and economic ideas fathered them. They are the impatient ones. All are driven by restlessness and a consuming desire for improvement. They fight among themselves as to whether their countries should be capitalistic or socialistic, but they agree on the need for erecting new and different nations on the framework of the old.

The intellectuals and the professionals—the lawyers and doctors and engineers—are the most vocal of this group. They are the leaders in the new middle and upper classes. Some become presidents, as in Argentina and Venezuela today. The new industrialists and the modern merchants make common cause with them in raising tariff barriers and in establishing what they feel are the economic perquisites of nationhood. Newly arrived foreign investors are a special part of this entrepreneurial group. Companies such as Sears, Roebuck and Co. and Kaiser Industries Corp., bring with them more than the latest production techniques. They bring also advanced public relations notions, and most importantly the conviction that purchasing from local suppliers helps build internal markets as well as safety of investment. Such convictions and techniques help feed the growth of the new middle economic and social groups.

And as always where modern industries implant themselves, trade unionism begins to develop, and the unions likewise are vociferous and restless. Although unionism is by and large more political than economic in Latin America—and not as yet a mature and responsible force—the social impact of organized labor has already been strongly felt in Argentina, Brazil, Cuba, Chile, Venezuela and Mexico, and it will certainly grow in the future.

Labor, industry and commerce and the intellectuals often speak with opposing voices. But they are all vociferous. They are all impatient. They all clamor restlessly for progress.

THE RESISTERS, the second category, are the traditionalists. They resist for varied reasons, ranging from protection of their economic interests to mere fear of change. The Hispanophile fears an invasion of alien values. He usually allies himself with those among the religious traditionalists who equate industrialism with the feared liberal Protestantism of the Anglo-Saxon world. Sometimes the old-type foreign investor joins in the resisting group. His enterprises usually are in farming and mining, and he fears nationalism, state interventionism and an unruly labor force.

The hacienda owners symbolize the resisters. Historically they are the richest men in Latin America. They fear they will lose their estates, or that their work force will leak away to the attractions of the city. The hacienda is much more than a large agricultural property owned by one family and worked by tenant farmers. It is a social and economic system unto itself, a system that has held back both the democratic and the economic development of Latin America. Although today the hacienda system is not as widespread as it was, it still exists throughout much of Latin America. In the two countries where it has been repudiated, Mexico and Bolivia, it was overthrown only by revolution.

I do not include the Roman Catholic Church in many countries among the resisters, though historically it has been allied with the forces of conservatism. In the 19th century, as new governments emerged and attempted to pattern themselves on French and U.S. constitutional precepts, a wave of anticlericalism swept over Latin America. Violence erupted against the priests and bishops. In one sense the political history of the 19th century in Latin America can be written in terms of anticlerical "liberalism" versus proclerical "conservatism." This division still exists in theory in Colombia today, for example, with the church involved in the political division between the two parties. (We were jestingly told that the Conservatives go to mass at 6 A.M. and the Liberals at 8 A.M.) A young student political leader of the National University in Bogotá insisted on discussing this with us. He reported, "The church is improving. It is now much more advanced in its thinking, often far more advanced than some of our politicians. It is even occasionally to be found in the vanguard of social progress." Here one sees grudging respect for the social leadership of the church even from a young agitator.

Elsewhere in Latin America the church has established its political prestige with liberal leaders by taking a strong position in favor of land reform. Further, in recent years it has stood against dictatorships in Argentina, Colombia and Venezuela. Now it is courageously resisting the Castro leadership in Cuba. This political leadership has little to do with the church's continuing importance as a religious institution. Even many bitter anticlericals continue to attend mass sporadically, send their children to the church for religious instruction and confirmation and consecrate life's most important events within religion's fold.

A major political problem in Latin America is to adjust the legitimate aspirations of the vociferous restless ones to the often justified and legitimate fears of the resisters. It is the noise of their clash which most often echoes in the hemisphere's newspapers, north and south.

THE SILENT ONES are the third big group. They have no voice in political affairs. They have little hope and usually no desire for any eventful incorporation into the life of their larger communities. The most obvious members are the Indians, held within their villages by their separate languages and dress and social usages. The integrity of their culture is under constant attack from without, and their days as distinct cultural units are numbered. A few national political movements have sought to identify Indian values with the emerging nation-states, with results dramatically visible in the plastic arts and literature. The famous new campus of the National University in Mexico City is one of the best examples of this mingling of artistic blood streams.

The peons, products of the hacienda system, are among the silent and voiceless. Rooted to the soil, most of them illiterate and hopelessly in debt, they comprise a potential source of unrest.

More explosive potentially, however, are their cousins, the silent lost people of the cities. Living in appalling slums, unlettered, performing the most menial tasks, they are feeling the first pangs of desire for a better life for themselves and their children. As yet they remain inert. Despite their occasional participation in unorganized street riots, they continue for the present to be uncertain fodder for the demagogue. Most prominently in Argentina during the regime of Juan Perón—but also in Brazil during the dictatorship of Getúlio Vargas—this group did gain political importance. How the "shirtless ones" finally arrive at political integration will be a significant part of the drama of Latin America's future.

These great rents in Latin-American society are stitched together by custom and habit so that life may continue. The stability of such institutions as the family, the church and the circle of friends makes for a set of complex personal loyalties which often override the divisive effects of social or political and economic conflict. There are many shock absorbers between the *fulanos de tal* (the John Does of Latin America) and the deep upheavals through which their countries are passing as they draw themselves into their own versions of modern life.

Militarism

These rips and tears of course harbor political and social infections, such as Communism, which batten on wrenching change. Notorious among these infections is militarism. Class dissension is an invitation to the military to convert itself into governing authority. The traditional pattern is called *caudillismo*, which means bossism, the rule of a strong man, himself either a military figure or backed by the military. This practice is still common in the less-developed countries, and was almost universal in the 19th century.

Contemporary manifestations of a new type of militarism are to be seen. Indeed, one of the surprises of my visit to Latin America was the fact that some defend the role of the military, at least potentially. They argue that the military forms a stabilizing factor in politics; that the armed forces teaches good health habits, basic literacy and even useful trades to young rural recruits; they foresee that military organizations can be directed into a Latin-American equivalent of our U.S. Civilian Conservation Corps, to be used for road building and other constructive purposes. Both in Venezuela and in Argentina the military have very recently acted to overthrow the *caudillos* (Marcos Pérez Jiménez and Juan Perón) whom they themselves originally backed. Then, guiding the country through a period of tutelage, military leaders in both cases have supervised quite honest elections and turned their countries over to the rule of civilian presidents. The Mexican army also participated in the same evolution some years ago. Laudable as are these three examples, it remains obvious that so long as a social system permits military control, so long will democracy remain an unattainable ideal.

Some of the problems growing from militarism and the armaments competition among various countries will be discussed later on.

A Basic Schizophrenia

Throughout Latin America a feudal 16th-century way of life is being thrust into a 20th-century world. Many Latin Americans (I have called these The Resisters) would like to keep and enjoy the way of life that has been handed down to them, the ease, the unhurried pace, the enjoyment of a romantic past. But many more want what the modern world has to offer, great cities, good roads and automobiles, the latest scientific gadgets—these I have called The Vociferous Ones. Indeed, many of the powerful old families now would have the best of both worlds, the patronal, seigniorial society and the industrial and egalitarian one. Many still refuse to concede that they cannot have both.

The Vociferous Ones and The Resisters find at least one outlet in common. This is criticism and mistrust of the United States. Uncle Sam is easy to blame for apparent troubles. Yet while "Yanqui imperialism" is feared, at the same time the United States is accused of paying too much attention to Europe and Asia and not enough to Latin America. In Rio de Janeiro, a leading Brazilian said to me, "You rebuilt the roads of Italy for nothing. You gave her the money under the Marshall Plan to rebuild her railroads. Yet you won't lend us—we who supported you loyally during World War II and in Korea—you won't lend us the money to build our power plants and dredge our harbors and put in our highways."

> [A respected United States ambassador told me that the key problem of the United States is "to get ourselves out of a position of responsibility for the failure of various Latin-American countries to develop their own economies."]

But what are our actual responsibilities and opportunities in the role of leadership that history has thrust upon us, and

Credit: René Burri—Magnum Photos

An awed family of Brazilians visiting their "city of tomorrow"—Brasília.

just how do they differ from what the Latin Americans expect of us? These I seek to examine in the closing section of this book in which I discuss U.S. policy for Latin America. First and foremost, I am convinced that what is most needed is far greater mutual understanding between the United States and Latin America. I like to hope this book may make some contribution to that end.

The Developing Voice of Latin America

For 400 years Latin America has absorbed the cultural stimuli and the manufactured products of the western world. Commercially, it has returned little more than commodities—gold, silver, copper, coffee, sugar, bananas. Now, it is accelerating its cultural contributions and the individual countries are turning into highly individualistic nations, each with its own particular manner of viewing the world, each able more than ever before to speak to the remainder of the western peoples in understandable and yet original terms. In painting, music, literature, architecture, as well as political example, Latin America is developing a voice of authority, of universality within diversity. It is demonstrating that, as the underdeveloped nations join in with the rest of the western world, they will increase not merely our material wealth but our richness of appreciation and of knowledge and insight. The excitements of fresh discovery lie ahead for them—and for us.

The world is pressing in on the once neglected countries of Latin America. And the world must now accustom itself to being pressured in return. The voice of Latin America is beating upon us in a mighty chorus—a chorus less and less discordant and with ever-increasing harmony. For our part, we must learn better how to listen and how to convert the pressures upon us into the leadership the hemisphere and the world seek from us.

2

The Struggle Upward Toward the Sun

After four centuries of conquest, colonization and *caudillos*, the people of Latin America are awakening to the challenge of modern life. The "revolution of rising expectations," in Governor Stevenson's great phrase, is taking hold. But their aspirations will not be satisfied by economic development alone. The former president of Costa Rica, José Figueres, told me that the Latin-American peoples "are more concerned with freedom than they are with economic development." He is at least partly right. He was wholly right when he declared that the great issue of Latin America is that of "dormant peoples struggling upward toward the sun, toward a better life." He placed political liberty and political democracy high among the values of his "better life."

Crisólogo Larralde, the leader of the People's Radical party in Argentina, which polled the biggest vote in the 1960 election, flatly told us that there is too much talk about economic development. He urged Governor Stevenson and me, on our return to the United States, to speak more of the "fight of ideas."

Such an ordering of values is most hopeful. The comments of

Figueres and Larralde represent a tradition ingrained among Latin-American intellectuals, a tradition that means that Latin Americans will not easily trade away their freedom for a mess of totalitarian economic promises. At the same time, we of the United States would be foolish to underrate the degree of interdependence between economic development and political freedom. In Latin America the first has become a vital factor in the second.

Because of its booming population, Latin America must develop very fast, economically, in order to stay where it is. Birth control is not favored in these Catholic countries. With the help of government programs fighting disease and high infant mortality, from 1920 to 1956 Latin America's population more than doubled. Average life expectancy is still only 45 years, however, compared with more than 70 in the U.S. Currently, the over-all rate of population increase is a staggering 2.6% each year—one of the highest rates in the world. A projection made by the Pan American Union gives Latin America a 1975 population of 293,400,000 and the United States only 217,000,000. If the present rate of growth holds up, in the next 25 to 30 years Latin America's total population will nearly double from its present 198,000,000 to close to 400,000,000. This will be a considerably greater population than the total for the U.S. and Canada. Such a skyrocketing growth could create acute problems for a stable economy; for the underdeveloped, economically volatile countries of Latin America it can produce political chaos.

If the hoped for economic evolution does not materialize soon, the economic problems resulting from the population explosion may erupt in full-scale social revolution, not just in one country, as in Cuba, but in many. Eduardo Santos, former President of Colombia and now its leading publisher, commented, "As things are going now, the greatest outburst in history is brewing in Latin America. Economic aid isn't the sole cure." The grave question of the coming decade is whether the people of Latin America, without violence or revolution, can learn to achieve the goals of social justice and human dignity, and can be helped to achieve them, by evolutionary, democratic means. Such means include, first and foremost, rapid and constructive economic development.

The Politico-Economic Pattern

The first impact of the pattern of Latin-American political life is on its economic life. This political pattern is complex—it is different for each country—with none like that of the United

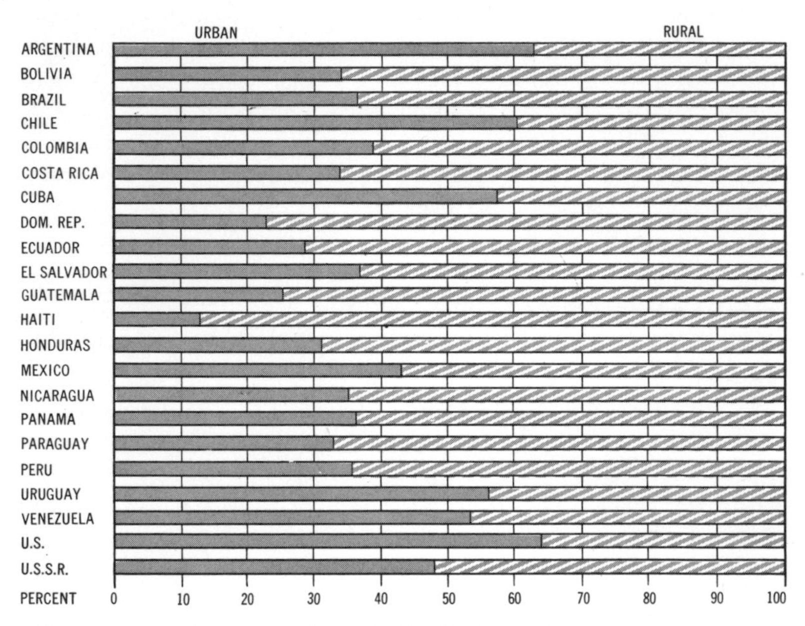

Percentages of urban and rural distribution of population in Latin America, U.S. and U.S.S.R. (*Sources:* Most recent available census reports from individual countries)

States. Mexico, for example, is autocratically ruled by a single party. Feudal and monied aristocracies are powerful in Peru, Ecuador and elsewhere. Dictatorships smother potential opposition in Nicaragua, the Dominican Republic and Paraguay—and now in Cuba.

Governor Stevenson and I were impressed by the personality and ability of most of the political leaders we met. I believe today's Latin-American political leaders stack up with leaders to be found in most countries throughout the world. I refer to men we met such as President López Mateos and Minister of Education Jaime Torres Bodet of Mexico; former Pres. Galo Plaza of Ecuador; Pres. Alberto Lleras Camargo of Colombia; Premier Pedro Beltrán of Peru; Pres. Jorge Alessandri of Chile; Pres. Arturo Frondizi and Minister of the Economy Alvaro Alsogaray of Argentina; former Pres. Juscelino Kubitschek of Brazil; and Pres. Rómulo Betancourt of Venezuela. As individuals, they hold differing views on politics and economics, just as members of our own congress hold differing views. But no one can doubt their dedication. They will make mistakes and some of them will follow policies of which the U.S. will disapprove; but they are the kind of men who can provide the leadership Latin America needs, leadership that can move in the direction of both economic development and political democracy. This new postwar group of political leaders is one ground for hope about Latin America's future.

THE PLIGHT OF THE INDIANS.—Both politically and economically, the central test these men face is how to lift the level of life of the "submerged third" of the population, and most importantly that of the Indian population. How can the Indian be introduced into the 20th century? This one question puts the political-economic problem of much of Latin America in its sharpest focus.

So long as he was able to make a living from the land, the Indian remained passive. For decades without number he has been drafted into revolutionary armies and has fought to overthrow dictators. Seldom has he asked for or received his share of the rewards.

Fertility is the quality most desired in an Indian woman. Traditionally, in order to raise three children, she has had to bear eight or ten. Now modern medicine is keeping her children alive. Thus it is highly likely that the number of Indians will double within ten years. This steady increase in Indian population means that the land is becoming progressively insufficient to produce the food needed for life. The Indians thus migrate to the cities. Already overcrowded, the cities that beckon so temptingly offer the migrant Indian little but poverty, filth and disease. This poses bitter choices.

Governor Stevenson and I visited the slums of Lima, Bogotá, Rio de Janeiro, Santiago and Caracas. Somehow those in Lima seemed the most degraded of all—perhaps because we had just had lunch at the Club Nacional, one of the most luxurious men's clubs in the world. Within a five-minute drive of this citadel of Lima's wealth we reached the most execrable slums I have seen in this hemisphere, vast stretches of one-room brick and mud huts in which people live in utter squalor, without plumbing and surrounded by filth and pigs—and empty beer bottles.

In this particular shantytown about 1,000 families—by no means all of them Indians—live in huts built on old garbage dumps, some going back 350 years. In the least squalid part of the slum we found a small wooden shack which serves as a church functioning under an extraordinary French priest who devotes his life to these "lost people." He showed us a room which serves as a kind of community center, then took us to the worst section. This was crowded with hundreds of pigs—underfoot everywhere—burrowing for garbage. The priest told us that about 5,000 pigs roam through this slum, an average of about five per family.

The migrant Indians, searching for the will-o'-the-wisp of a better life, cannot find it in slums such as this. Peru's Premier Beltrán told us "the way to keep the Indians in the mountains is to make their lives better there." Yet the task of helping the Indians help themselves turns out to be much greater than one would expect. Alberto Giesecke, onetime Rector of the University of Cuzco and a student of Indian culture and history, told us about the experience of a U.S. Point Four team in Peru which moved into a village and decided to teach the Indians to boil water in order to cut down on illness and disease. After almost two years, only 11 of the 200 families in the village had been persuaded to boil their water. He told us also of a not un-

Credit: Magnum Photos

Governor Stevenson and Senator Benton talking with Father Pablo Protain in a slum of Lima, Peru. In the background hogs feed on a garbage dump.

usual experience near Cuzco where a Point Four program had succeeded in doubling an Indian village's potato crop in just one year. The Indians were overjoyed and held a fiesta for eight days —during which they ate all the potatoes! They didn't even leave enough seed potatoes to plant the following year.

But there are brighter spots of hope. A project headed by Allan Holmberg, an anthropologist of Cornell university, trained 2,500 Peruvian Indians on a large publicly owned hacienda to take over its management. Five years later, productivity was up 600%, and 400 children were being educated where none had been before. There are now nine similar projects operating in Peru. A United Nations report says the Indians are "highly trainable."

Vance Rogers, director of the U.S. Point Four Program in Peru, asked, "As the Indians move from the Stone Age, will they move toward the Communists?" He told us that he thought the key to the success of such projects as Holmberg's is the extension of small credits to the Indian farmers for seeds and fertilizer. He told us, as had former President Plaza of Ecuador, that "the Indians always pay the money back." Rogers is persuaded that "how the Indians will emerge will depend on the economic opportunities accorded them." Most highborn Peruvians of "the oligarchy" tend to ignore the problem, but Premier Beltrán recognizes it and is anxious to take steps to meet it.

Latin America's rural Indians have yet to learn—and have yet to win—the opportunity to use the ballot box to improve their lot. In Ecuador and Peru the Indian must pass a literacy test in order to vote. I heard one rising young Peruvian politician, asked if he spoke Quechua (one of the two main Indian languages), reply that it made no difference whether he did or did not, because those that spoke it had no vote.

THE BROADER PROBLEM.—I think Governor Stevenson phrased the broader problem aptly when he remarked at a dinner in Rio de Janeiro, "One of the great issues throughout Latin America today is whether the goal of democracy will prevail; will we see the triumph of government by the consent of the governed?" The Governor was thinking not only of the Indian but of all

Credit: Standard Oil Co. (N.J.)

Indian farmers of Colombia planting potatoes in the tundra at an elevation of 12,000 ft. in the Cordillera Oriental. Between 1930 and 1960 Colombia's industry rose 66%, agricultural output only 14%.

the voiceless governed—those who are not educated or encouraged or permitted to take part in political life.

The famous Argentine economist Raúl Prebisch, of whom I shall have much to say, touched on the relevance of this broader problem for U.S. foreign economic policy when he argued that the major goal in our own national interest as well as Latin America's is to improve the living standards of the lower half of the population. This can best be achieved only by the type of economic development that is advanced by better use of each country's basic natural resources—mineral, agricultural and human. The problem for U.S. policy is how best to exert our leadership, and how best to allocate available U.S. resources toward this end. Our aim should not be primarily to foster U.S. private industry and initiative, important as this is. Our aim should be to assist the Latin countries to improve the living standards of their people and thus to help them generate the climate which breeds freedom and democracy.

The Pattern of the Struggle

Latin America is coming into industrialization at a time when technology elsewhere is already in an advanced state. The Communists say to Latin America: "Follow the Soviet system and you will catch up rapidly." Should we of the United States counter by saying: "Follow our free-enterprise, free-market system and you will achieve both personal freedom and a high standard of living?"

The practical alternatives are not that stark. No Latin-American country has ever had a laissez-faire, capitalistic system in any full sense, nor has any had a sustained system of full state socialism. The normal Latin-American cultural tendency is to be statist; ours in the U.S. is the reverse. Their definition of free enterprise does not include the element of individual responsibility as does the Anglo-American tradition.

The promotion of industrialization has been a governmental function in all Latin-American countries. Since the great depres-

Table I.–General Data on the Twenty Latin-American Republics

Country	*Area (sq. mi.)*	*Population (most recent estimate)*	*Population density per sq. mi.*	*Annual rate of increase (1953–58)*	*Capital*	*Head of Government 1961*
Argentina	1,072,746	20,959,100	19.5	1.9	Buenos Aires	Arturo Frondizi (President)
Bolivia	424,162	3,416,000	8.1	1.4	La Paz/Sucre	Victor Paz Estenssoro (President)
Brazil	3,287,195	66,302,271	20.1	2.4	Brasília	Jânio Quadros (President)
Chile	286,396	7,551,000	26.4	2.5	Santiago	Jorge Alessandri Rodríguez (President)
Colombia	439,512	14,131,660	32.2	2.2	Bogotá	Alberto Lleras Camargo (President)
Costa Rica	19,695	1,125,828	57.2	4.0	San José	Mario Echandi Jiménez (President)
Cuba	44,218	6,743,000	152.5	1.9	Havana	Fidel Castro (Premier)
Dominican Republic	18,703	4,070,108	217.6	3.5	Ciudad Trujillo	Coalition between Lt. Gen. Rafael L. Trujillo Molina, Jr., and Joanquín Balaguer (President)
Ecuador	105,684	4,298,449	40.7	2.9	Quito	José Velasco Ibarra (President)
El Salvador	8,260	2,613,000	316.3	3.5	San Salvador	Col. César Yanes Urías, Ranking Officer of a six-man junta
Guatemala	42,042	3,759,000	89.4	3.0	Guatemala City	Gen. Miguel Ydígoras Fuentes (President)
Haiti	10,714	3,505,000	327.1	1.2	Port-au-Prince	François Duvalier (President)
Honduras	43,277	1,950,000	45.1	3.3	Tegucigalpa	Ramón Villeda Morales (President)
Mexico	760,335	34,625,903	45.5	2.9	México City	Adolfo López Mateos (President)
Nicaragua	57,143	1,450,349	25.4	3.4	Managua	Luis Somoza Debayle (President)
Panamá	28,753	1,053,000	36.6	2.9	Panamá City	Roberto F. Chiari (President)
Paraguay	157,047	1,728,292	11.0	2.3	Asunción	Gen. Alfredo Stroessner (President)
Peru	496,222	10,857,000	21.9	2.5	Lima	Manuel Prado y Ugarteche (President)
Uruguay	72,152	2,800,000	38.8	1.3	Montevideo	Benito Nardone (President)
Venezuela	352,142	6,709,000	19.1	3.0	Caracas	**Rómulo Betancourt (President)**

sion, moreover, Latin-American credit has been bad on the exchanges of the world. Thus governments have been called on to guarantee external loans for business development. This in itself has deeply involved governments in the industrialization process.

A further basic factor limiting private or free enterprise is that many modern industries, to be reasonably efficient, must operate on a large scale. Effective markets in Latin America are at present relatively small almost everywhere; for most countries, only one or two factories are required in any given field to supply present demand. This fact creates incentives toward monopoly and high prices. One major antidote for limited demand, over and above the basic need to increase purchasing power, is the development of a common market throughout Latin America; such a market free of trade barriers among the Latin countries will encourage competition and volume production.

It seems clear to me that the United States, as a government, will be wise if it seeks to avoid being doctrinaire about economic policies in its attempts to help Latin America with its development. The U.S. must learn to be flexible in its approach to the differing Latin-American countries. Here is where ideas can count for more than money. More of this later.

One collateral benefit can accrue to us if we consciously try to figure out which economic or developmental pattern can work best in each Latin-American country. The knowledge so derived could help guide us in other underdeveloped areas of the world as they begin to face the same problems.

RAÚL PREBISCH.—One of the most brilliant social scientists in Latin America is Raúl Prebisch, director of the United Nations Economic Commission for Latin America (ECLA) with headquarters in Santiago, Chile. Formerly head of the Central bank in Argentina, Prebisch has been the leader in promoting a common market. This has won him the sobriquet "the Jean Monnet of South America." A number of my friends had told me that a visit with him would be one of the significant opportunities of my journey. I told him he was as famous among my friends as the Andes. Governor Stevenson and I spent two hours with him at his office, and I was fortunate enough to be invited to dinner twice at his home.

Prebisch posed the key question about economic development in Latin America, "Why is the rate of growth so weak? At present it is running only about 1% per year." His answer: "One, the rate of savings is low; two, the land tenure system is a terrible handicap; three, the continent suffers from lack of trained manpower and insufficient use of manpower; and four, everywhere there is misuse of capital." This is a heavy indictment and it poses a heavy series of problems.

Prebisch continued, "Look at the way the high-income groups live in Latin America. They have all the advantages of the past and the present." He argued that Latin America needs more steeply graduated taxes on income so that a bigger proportion of high-income money can be used for government-designated aims.

[Of course, I emphatically agree. Any North American in a high tax bracket who visits Latin America is almost sure to resent the fact that in many countries the rich seem to avoid taxes and yet they and their officials seek and expect grants and loans from the U.S. And one may add that under the heading of "foreign capital" needed for economic development in Latin America can be included a substantial part of the capital wealthy Latin Americans keep in banks in Switzerland, the United States and other countries, or which they put in speculative investments abroad, for example in Florida real estate. Victor L. Urquidi, Mexican economist formerly with the ECLA, in reply to a question at the annual conference of the Canadian Institute on Public Affairs in 1960, estimated the total of such "idle" Latin American capital in other countries as possibly from $3 to $4 billion. Part of this money was "stashed away" in advance by dictators and their associates who have been deposed in recent years. But the greater part belongs to exporters of coffee and other commodities who prefer to keep their dollars abroad rather than put them to work in their own countries. These billions seeking safety abroad seem to undercut some of the cogency of the Latin-American argument in favor of "soft" grants and loans from the U.S. government.]

Prebisch went on to explain that in "many Latin-American countries the feeling is ingrained that the free play of economic forces" will do the developmental job. Thus "economic planning is not always easily accepted." To many people (The Resisters), he said, state intervention or planning seems synonomous with agrarian reform, with higher taxes and structural changes in the economy that will unleash new social forces. Prebisch spoke of the feeling of frustration in the younger generation. He pointed out that only a greater rate of growth can provide greater economic opportunities for "the dynamic younger elements who are destined to be the leaders." Without such opportunities, the frustration can boil up into political dissension.

Prebisch asked a pair of questions: "Why don't progressive elements in Latin America believe in the United States? Why doesn't the United States attract them to the support of its policies?" He reminded us that the progressive elements in Latin America had believed in Franklin Roosevelt. He said that unhappily their faith in the U.S. has now been lost. Such groups, said Prebisch, want to duplicate in Latin America many of the things the United States has done—they want to control their monopolies; they would like to have strong free labor unions; they are eager to foster land reform; they would like to imitate our system of taxation. He asked why—instead of lining up our policies to support such reforms in Latin America—why does United States policy concentrate so largely on the importance of "foreign private initiative?"

If more credit is made available to Latin America, Prebisch told us—and he means credits to Latin-American governments not only for health, education, roads and public utilities, but also on occasion for government-operated industries—this can produce an enormous boost in private enterpreneurship. He conceded enthusiastically that there are many things only foreign private capital can do, and said further that he could not possibly exaggerate the past and potential importance of U.S. private industry in the development of the economies of Latin America. But there are many urgent needs to which it cannot be expected to contribute. Of course I would personally strongly favor a policy whereby Latin-American governments, when government capital and intervention is necessary to begin with, divest themselves of ownership as soon as private enterprise is able and willing to take over.

Seven Economic Problems

Everywhere we went—and notably among political leaders—discussion of Latin America's economic future revolved mostly around four themes: land reform and housing; industrialization; foreign capital and foreign technical aid; and inflation. The role of labor unions was a fifth though lesser theme; the common market as well as Operation "Pan America," proposed by former President Kubitschek of Brazil, provided a sixth conversational gambit; and the problem of export commodity prices was a seventh. I shall now touch on each of these briefly, though not in this exact order.

Land Reform, Land Use and Housing

Despite the present trend toward industrialization, Latin America's economy is still based largely on agriculture. The urgent need is a great rise in the efficiency of the agricultural worker and the owner of the land. Agricultural technology has not materially improved, as it has in the U.S., and unlike the United States, production for internal consumption has not kept pace with population during the past 20 years. The great emphasis on industrial development, which has attracted millions to the cities, has left many countries with actual food shortages. Gov. Carvalho Pinto of the state of São Paulo, Brazil, contended that the economic effort in his country is out of focus because of the failure to put sufficient emphasis on agriculture. Further, he said that the failure of the Brazilian government to develop agriculture properly will still further accelerate migration to the cities—which in turn will prove most unhappy for the country.

This doubtless explains why a major point stressed by Prebisch is the need for better utilization of the land. Before we left Wash-

Cost of living index, selected years, 1951–59. (*Source:* United Nations Statistical Yearbook)

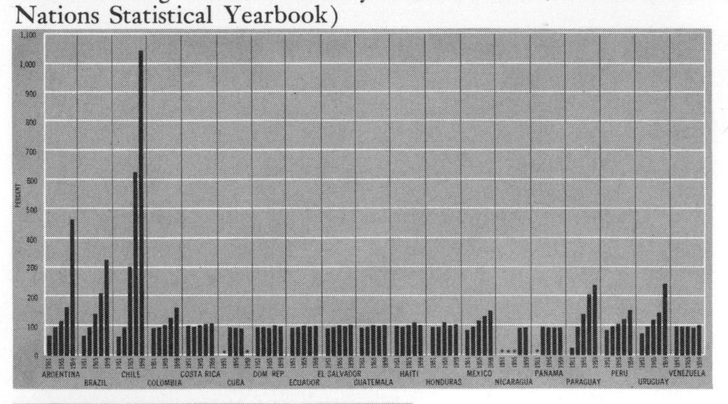

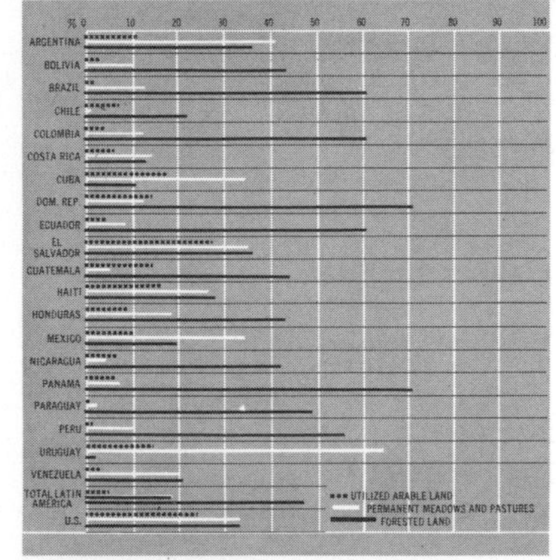

Land use showing (1) utilized arable land; (2) permanent meadows and pastures; (3) forested land. Also a comparison between total land use in Latin America and the U.S. (*Source:* United Nations Food and Agriculture Organization)

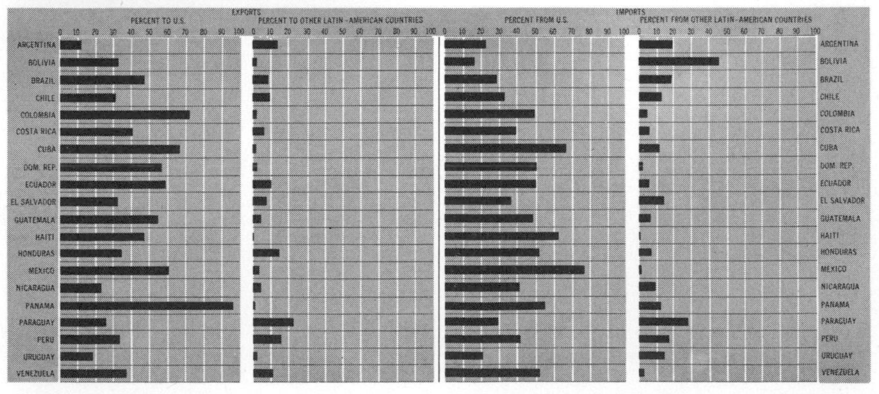

Exports and imports shown in terms of trade with the U.S. as contrasted to trade with other Latin American nations. (*Sources:* Encyclopaedia Britannica World Atlas; statistical reports from individual countries)

Credit: Secretaria de Estado das Relaçoes Exteriores

Brazilian coffee workers raking beans for drying in the sun. Brazil is one of 14 Latin American countries depending upon a single commodity for one-half or more of its export earnings.

ington we had been told by U.S. State Department experts that land reform may well be the central economic problem of Latin America. There are so many misconceptions of just what the term "land reform" means that perhaps a definition is in order. The *Encyclopaedia Britannica* has this to say about land reform:

> It usually means a specific, integrated-action program to bring about more effective control and use of land for the direct benefit of the agricultural population and for the indirect benefit of the community as a whole. For example, land reform includes, without widespread dissent, the redistribution of agricultural land among existing or new owners, including consolidation or subdivision; development or settlement of holdings; adjustment of rental charges; compulsory reimbursement of costs incurred by the tenant for improvements made on the land he cultivates; increase in the security of tenure; adjustment of policy and procedure in the taxation of agricultural land; and the adjudication and registration of land and water titles.
>
> But land reform may also embrace improvements in the entire agrarian structure, such as agricultural or general education of rural populations; improvement of working conditions and the social status of all classes of farm workers; improvement of farm credit conditions; the establishment of industries or co-operative societies for the production, processing and marketing of farm products and for the purchase of farm supplies; technical advice to farmers; and numerous other types of farm community or individual services.

Although Latin America has been an agricultural economy for centuries, only 5% of its total area is in tillage or under tree crops, as compared with 24% in the United States. About 65% of Latin America's population still is rural and more than half its labor force is employed in agriculture, but they produce only 24% of the gross product. President Lleras Camargo of Colombia told us that in the last 30 years his country's industry has grown 66% while agricultural output has risen only 14%. He said that Colombia has plenty of available land and can institute a program of land reform without taking land from its owners. He added, "This is where Colombia needs international credit, but unfortunately bankers feel that the best creditors are manufacturers who can be quickly productive. Nothing is more urgently needed [in Colombia] than a land resettlement program." President Lleras Camargo is eager to encourage the refugees in the cities' slums to move back to the land.

In Chile, where 21% of all the irrigated land in the most valuable areas is lying fallow, President Alessandri told us that his land-reform program, like that of President Lleras Camargo, does not contemplate expropriating or breaking up the big private estates but is based on redistribution of land already in the control of the government. He explained that much of this land had been "very badly exploited" by government managers who have controlled the votes of peasants living on it. President Alessandri wants to take this land from government bureaucrats who have failed to develop it and turn it over to people who will.

Chile's basic agronomic problem, however, springs partly from the history of its settlement. Lands in the centre of the country, developed early by Spaniards, are divided into relatively large estates which grow crops ordinarily raised by extensive cultivation on small farms, for example, grapes. Lands to the south, developed later by central European immigrants, are held in relatively small plots devoted to crops ordinarily grown on extensive holdings, for example, wheat. This is in the reverse order of what would prove most productive.

In Peru.—In Lima, Premier Beltrán explained that there is plenty of land in Peru, and there is no need to take the land of the big hacienda owners. The surplus land is beyond the Andes and is presently inaccessible. He wants to open it up with good roads for the Indians. One U.S. expert told us this land is definitely inferior to the western land of the big haciendas of Peru's ruling "400 families." In both Chile and Peru the big haciendas are increasing their productivity at a rate too slow to meet the demand of the cities for foodstuffs; further, they characteristically produce export products, such as cotton and sugar in Peru and wine grapes in Chile.

In Ecuador.—Former Pres. Galo Plaza drove us through the

beautiful valleys of the Sierra of Ecuador and pointed out some of the impressive old gates that led to the ruined haciendas of the past. He told us that this "breakup" of the big estates has not been accomplished by any legislative reform but strictly by economic processes. It is no longer necessary for Ecuadorians, he said, to hang on to land for purposes of prestige. The new professional groups, often the descendants of the old landowners, do not feel they need land. But the landlord tradition is still strong, and many of the Indian farmers are legally required to make annual payments to landlords, such as a pig each Christmas. Thus the Indians do not actually have full and valid title. Such title is what Plaza wants to achieve for them.

IN ARGENTINA the land problem is of a different order from that in most of Latin America. In Buenos Aires I had a most interesting discussion with Federico Pinedo, Argentina's Minister of Finance in 1933 and again in the early days of World War II. Pinedo disagreed sharply with the statement made to us in Washington about land reform. He told us that when it is more economic to break up the big estates, this will come about automatically. He pointed out that in the United States over the last 20 years the average size of farms has grown and the number of tenant farmers increased.

Later in Buenos Aires we had luncheon with Guillermo Klein, Secretary of State in the Ministry of the Treasury. He agreed with Pinedo that the big landed estates in Argentina were not an important problem. He said that they are often far more efficient than the smaller units and pointed out that the big estates were essential for efficient cattle breeding. But he assured us that the big estates will be broken up in time. He told us of the Argentinian law of 1870 that compels the distribution of all property upon death—in equal parts to each child. Only 20% of the property is at the free disposal of the parent. So, unless a family corporation is formed to keep the estate together, it is automatically broken up by death.

There seems to be little clamor by farm people in Argentina for land; Argentine farming and cattle raising employ relatively few people, and many of these are migratory workers. But agricultural research is greatly needed, as it is throughout the continent.

Indeed, this is probably agriculture's greatest need. In the U.S. we spend $75,000,000 or $80,000,000 annually on such research and our great rise in output-per-man-hour stems largely from the agricultural experimental stations and agricultural colleges. A few million dollars a year spent on agricultural research in Latin America should greatly step up productivity.

We spent a day at one of the ranches of International Packers, Ltd., in Brazil, a U.S.-owned and operated packing company that in 1959 did a $400,000,000 business. A. Thomas Taylor of Chicago, its chairman, told me that the eradication of foot-and-mouth disease in Argentina would step up beef production 25% to 30%. He has scientists in Germany investigating new vaccines, and has discussed the problem with President Frondizi. Here, it seems to me, is the kind of problem that can be solved. And anything that will offer a 30% increase in productivity in so basic an industry as Argentine beef is indeed revolutionary. It is worth tremendous effort.

LAND DEVELOPMENT.—In most of Latin America the problem runs far deeper than securing land for the peasant farmers. It includes helping them develop the land. And this too calls for action by the government. Much of the land, for example a large part of the Brazilian northeast, the coastal deserts of Peru and Chile, the dry mountain regions of Bolivia and Peru and the plains of Colombia and Venezuela, cannot be farmed efficiently without irrigation. Few Latin-American governments today can find the funds for large-scale irrigation projects. Further, if isolated agricultural communities of Latin America are to be brought into contact with markets, large numbers of new roads must be built. Brigadier José Vicente de Faria Lima, the Minister of Public Works in the state of São Paulo told us that this is the key to agricultural development throughout Brazil. He said that in 1935 in his huge and rich state there were only 700-odd kilometers of paved highway. By contrast, in the last two and a

Table II.–Economics and Trade of the Latin-American Republics

Country	*Gross national product** *(1957 or 1958)*	*Net U.S. economic aid (loans and grants) (1954–58)*	*Balance of foreign trade (1959)*
Argentina	$17,599,494,000	–$14,800,000	$16,000,000
Bolivia	263,400,000†	100,900,000	–5,400,000
Brazil	69,686,665,000	236,600,000	–92,000,000
Chile	3,531,000,000	35,600,000	84,000,000
Colombia	2,310,334,400	75,500,000	59,000,000
Costa Rica	368,480,000	26,900,000	–23,000,000
Cuba	2,556,000,000	17,800,000	25,000,000
Dominican Republic	649,600,000	1,500,000	12,462,000
Ecuador	800,040,000	20,400,000	45,000,000
El Salvador	506,800,000	5,100,000	13,000,000
Guatemala	638,300,000	58,600,000	–14,000,000
Haiti	325,000,000‡	42,300,000	–2,000,000
Honduras	343,400,000	9,700,000	8,000,000
Mexico	9,127,000,000	61,400,000	–251,000,000
Nicaragua	195,746,200§	11,100,000	–1,800,000
Panamá	367,200,000	14,500,000	–63,000,000
Paraguay	219,111,872‖	15,800,000	5,002,000
Peru	1,361,924,400	125,700,000	17,000,000
Uruguay	382,973,554¶	–5,800,000	–62,000,000
Venezuela	6,437,152,500	–5,600,000	961,468,000

*At market prices. †1955 Gross domestic product at market prices. ‡1955. §1950. ‖National income. ¶Value of manufacturing.

Per cent of export earnings from one commodity	*Per cent of export earnings from two commodities*	*Principal imports*
26 (Meat)	39 (Meat; wheat)	Crude materials, mineral fuels, machinery
62 (Tin)	71 (Tin; lead)	Food, machinery
58 (Coffee)	64 (Coffee; cacao)	Mineral fuels, food, machinery
66 (Copper)	76 (Copper; nitrates)	Transport equipment, chemicals, food
77 (Coffee)	92 (Coffee; petroleum)	Machinery and transportation equipment, iron and steel
51 (Coffee)	86 (Coffee; bananas)	Iron and steel, machinery, textiles
77 (Sugar)	83 (Sugar; tobacco)	Machinery, petroleum, iron and steel
48 (Sugar)	65 (Sugar; cacao)	Machinery, textiles
57 (Bananas)	75 (Bananas; coffee)	Machinery and transportation equipment, chemicals
72 (Coffee)	88 (Coffee, cotton)	Transportation equipment, mineral fuels, textiles
72 (Coffee)	85 (Coffee; bananas)	Mineral fuels, machinery, iron and steel
63 (Coffee)	80 (Coffee; sisal)	Wheat flour, textiles
51 (Bananas)	70 (Bananas; coffee)	Chemicals, machinery, iron and steel
25 (Cotton)	36 (Cotton; coffee)	Machinery, chemicals, mineral fuels
39 (Cotton)	73 (Coffee; cotton)	Chemicals, iron and steel, machinery
69 (Bananas)	72 (Bananas; cacao)	Iron and steel, chemicals, machinery
24 (Timber)	46 (Timber; meat)	Chemicals, wheat, machinery
23 (Cotton)	38 (Cotton; sugar)	Wheat, iron and steel, machinery
54 (Wool)	68 (Wool; meat)	Sugar, machinery, mineral fuels
92 (Petroleum)		Machinery, iron and steel, chemicals

half years 2,300 km. have been paved, bringing the state's total to 6,048 paved kilometers—more than eight times the total of 1935. But road building can be expensive and most of the Latin-American republics lack both the machinery and the funds for it. They also lack the leadership to induce the people to get started with their spare time and crude tools. Further, even after the roads, farmers must still have credit to enable them to buy farm machinery, seeds, fertilizer. Warehouses and silos must be built co-operatively, either on credit or at government expense.

Premier Beltrán cited one project in which Indians moved to the eastern side of the Andes. They learned quickly to produce $1,000,000 worth of agricultural products. But this had to be transported over the mountains on "men's backs" at a tremendous waste of time and manpower—and at an estimated cost of $300,000.

OUTSIDE AID.—Many Latin-American leaders say that land-reform programs can be carried out successfully provided the United States and the international lending agencies will make loans on a country-by-country basis to implement them. They believe that if loans or grants for this purpose are supplemented by technical assistance the peasants of Latin America will respond productively. In considering such a proposition I believe we of the U.S. must recognize that we are being asked for grants rather than ordinary loans—or, at best, very low-interest, long-term "soft" loans, repayable in local currencies. Ordinary loans for this proposal would not produce dollar earnings over a short-term period. The Latin-American countries already are straining to meet their balance-of-payment problems out of current income.

Again and again Governor Stevenson and I were warned that the alternative may be a series of Castrolike revolutions throughout the hemisphere, with mass expropriation of privately owned land. If this is a threat aimed at the U.S., and requiring action by us, then I reject its underlying assumption. The problem is much more an internal one for the political leaders in each country who must themselves deal with their landed aristocracies and hacienda owners.

Table III.—Transportation and Communications

Country	*Railroad mileage (mi.)*	*Highways improved (mi.)*	*Autos (1956 59)*	*News-papers (1955–57)*	*Radio stations (1956–59)*	*Tele-phones (1958)*
Argentina	27,630	31,580	364,500	346	78	1,223,593
Bolivia	1,468	2,826	11,600	6	40	19,909
Brazil	22,989	282,787*	446,300	235	593†	928,117
Chile	5,500	11,790	53,800	73	119	166,184
Colombia	1,801	5,708	81,200	37	120	247,298
Costa Rica	816	1,707	12,800	5	38	12,961
Cuba	3,432	2,158	159,200	58	160	170,092
Dominican Republic	816	3,800	9,500	6	50	16,592
Ecuador	698	3,000	6,300	24‡	54†	25,000
El Salvador	388	764	14,300	7	22	11,973
Guatemala	719	2,500	19,900	6	25§	11,717
Haiti	165	808	5,300	6	17‡	4,239
Honduras	800	337	5,100	6	20‡	5,862
Mexico	14,547	17,774	365,800	198	417	447,984
Nicaragua	250	1,242	9,300	10	29	7,000
Panamá	240	711	22,200	11	64	23,937
Paraguay	700	711	5,800	6	15‖	9,172
Peru	2,260	11,700	62,100	58	95	91,242
Uruguay	1,801	25,958*	47,300‡	12	85	135,777
Venezuela	698	8,054	186,000	32	71	158,575

*Includes unimproved roads. †1955. ‡1952. §1954. ‖1953.

One of the slogans of the Mexican revolution of 1910 was land reform. Yet in 1959, half a century later, President López Mateos, in the first year of his administration, distributed more land than at any time since 1942. The first 20 years of the revolution were convulsive, and cost hundreds of thousands of lives. This was the opening chapter. Today, 50% of all tillable Mexican land is said to be in communal holdings—with 20% more in small holdings. In most other Latin-American nations, present-day political leaders are children of the plantation system and still think in terms of dealing with the land without destroying the plantation. This is one reason why Castro's cry of land reform has such appeal to the Latin-American masses.

I do not wish to imply that the land-reform problem is exclusively rural and agricultural. Latin America's cities have erupted in recent years—the population of Bogotá, for example, has grown from 250,000 in 1940 to 1,500,000 in 1960. This is a principal cause of the slums I have described. The cities have been unable to cope adequately with the problems of sanitation, lighting and transportation. Naturally, the average level of housing has deteriorated.

Thus, in the declaration of Bogotá climaxing the Economic conference held in September 1960, measures for the improvement of housing and community facilities were placed second only to rural land reform in the listing of Latin America's needs. The need for urban and regional planning, and for creation of private agencies to finance home building, were given special emphasis. A $53,000,000 U.S. loan to Peru announced in 1960 is intended for use in low-cost housing as well as in rural land reform.

However, I left Latin America feeling that land reform and urban redevelopment are problems far more serious than some of the political leaders seemed willing to concede. When these leaders are once determined to act, they can do much for themselves. When they aggressively seek to help themselves, there is then a real opportunity, under present U.S. policy, for us to be helpful. Until then we can do little.

Industrialization

From 1950 to 1957, industrial production in Latin America increased 37%. This was appreciably better than the agricultural production increase of 26% but far below the area's potential. If the Latin-American economy is to prosper, the concept of industrialization must be made a reality. Its development in the larger countries of Argentina, Brazil, Chile, Colombia, Mexico and Venezuela has been under attempted forced draft since World War II, accelerated by a variety of fiscal measures and incentives. One form of incentive is government support of overvalued exchange rates. This has tended to reduce the cost of importing capital equipment for industrial purposes, as well as to reduce the cost of imports of raw materials, of fuel and spare parts needed to operate. Further, exchange controls in some countries have often been administered in such a way as to protect established domestic industry from the competition of foreign imports and of foreign factories which would otherwise be attracted to the country.

Other kinds of protection, such as tariff or government controls, are forms of forced draft which often end up as hurdles to progress. Many of the so-called industrialization laws that purport to invite expansion are actually designed to exclude new entrants to an industry. In many countries it has often been considered "unfair competition" for a foreign firm to enter with modern equipment which can produce at substantially lower prices. Thus the rate of industrial expansion has often been held down by the tactics of entrenched producers who hope to reserve an expanding market for themselves without having to improve their production techniques to meet competition.

Another element that tends to retard the expansion of industry is the inadequacy of electric power and transportation. These continue to be bottlenecks in industrial growth. In booming São Paulo, for example, we were told that there is a long waiting list of industrial firms unable to get into production or expand existing facilities until new power-generating capacities are provided. In the case of transportation, existing firms find that their rate of expansion depends upon widening the domestic market—which can be achieved only by substantial government investment in railways, highways and auxiliary services.

The growing realization of Latin industrialists that power and transportation are essential to their own growth has placed great pressure on governments to invest heavily in these fields. In Mexico, President López Mateos wants to double his country's electric capacity within the next six years and wants private investors to do half of this. Yet he flatly refuses to allow electric rates to go up. Thus private investors hold back; they will search elsewhere for a greater margin of profit on investments. During 1960, the two foreign power companies operating in Mexico sold out their holdings to Mexican interests.

THE ENTERPRISING SPIRIT.—If the sorry slums I described earlier are the blight of Latin-American cities, this blight is offset in part by the cities' amazing and unexpected energy and vitality. They are not the sleepy towns of O. Henry's stories of the banana republics. From Mexico City straight through Medellín, Bogotá, Santiago, Buenos Aires and São Paulo I was pleased and surprised at the general spirit of enterprise, the resourcefulness and business determination. This is the new spirit of a Latin America hell-bent on industrialization.

Governor Stevenson and I had lunch with the directors of the U.S. Chamber of Commerce of São Paulo, an outstanding group of U.S. businessmen. The vice-president for Brazil of an important U.S. corporation told us that theirs was a unique group of expatriate Americans. He said, "We are here—all of us—voluntarily; we're here because we are happier here than we would be in the United States; we feel we can achieve greater fulfillment here. We don't want to go home; we like it better here."

Emory Williams, president of the Brazilian Sears, Roebuck and Co. subsidiary, told me Sears had invested $15,000,000 in its Brazilian enterprise and has allowed its profits to accumulate until its investment is almost $20,000,000. Sears has not taken out of Brazil in dividends an average of 1½% on its investment. Though it is wholly owned by the parent company in Chicago, it has gone into business whole-hog with Brazilians. Thus, if I, as a U.S. entrepreneur operating in São Paulo, wanted to set up a company to manufacture refrigerators to sell to Sears, Williams would much rather deal with a Brazilian entrepreneur—"everything else being equal." Less than 1% of Sears's retail volume in São Paulo is being imported, and this includes imports from Europe as well as from North America. This illustrates how Sears is developing Brazilian initiative, enterprise—and profits.[1]

[1] I attended the lunch in Mexico City when Sears, Roebuck opened its first store in Latin America in 1947. By 1953 Sears was operating seven stores in Mexico. Its gross sales of over $15,000,000 made it one of the dozen largest private corporations in the country—and also one of the largest taxpayers. By 1953 Mexico-Sears was buying 80% of all its merchandise from more than 1,200 Mexican suppliers. It had given financial and technical assistance

At this luncheon I chatted also with Howard Mason, executive vice-president of Anderson, Clayton & Co. of Brazil. My long and close friendship with Will Clayton of Houston, who in 1945 was instrumental in bringing me into the State Department, gives me a special interest in this firm. Mason described his company's contribution to Brazil's economy. Anderson, Clayton & Co. did Brazilian business of around $90,000,000 in 1960. The biggest single American-owned business in Brazil, it deals largely in products based on vegetable oil—oleomargarine, peanut butter, salad oil and cooking oil. Mason said that Anderson, Clayton's total world business exceeded $1,000,000,000, of which the Brazilian subsidiary contributes a significant amount.

Mason thinks that the biggest problem the United States faces in Brazil is "to make our good points known." He thinks it is a public relations problem. (In other words, this experienced U.S. businessman is providing strong arguments for an increased budget and improved personnel for the United States Information Agency which I used to head. Mason feels that Americans should "mix much more with the Brazilians."

NEW INDUSTRIES.—A day or two later, accompanied by Hickman Price, Jr., director of the Brazilian Mercedes-Benz company, we drove through an area on the outskirts of São Paulo closely packed with modern factories. Price told us that this area had been a tropical jungle only five years ago. Next to the Mercedes-Benz plant was the Willys plant, which Price had established when he was in charge of overseas sales for Kaiser-Willys. Each of these plants employs around 6,000 people and does an annual volume of about $75,000,000. Fiat and Volkswagen also have plants in the São Paulo area.

---

to hundreds of these suppliers to help them learn to produce the wanted merchandise. By 1960, 97.4% of all goods sold in the retail outlets of Sears of Mexico were produced in Mexico; only 19 of the 3,051 employees of the company were non-Latin Americans. Sears, Roebuck provides a marvelous story of U.S. enterprise and initiative in Latin America, at their best both for Sears and for Latin America. This story is a great tribute to Gen. Robert E. Wood, the great business leader who headed Sears for a quarter century and who took it to Latin America.

The Mercedes-Benz story is a remarkable one which illustrates the financial opportunity in Brazil's inflationary boom economy. A Pole named Alfred Jurzykowski, who owned a series of chocolate plants in Poland before the war, escaped into Turkey in 1939 as a Polish officer. He had money on deposit in New York, Switzerland and elsewhere. He pyramided this money, first becoming a U.S. citizen and then a Brazilian. In 1946, when Germany was flat on its back, he signed a contract with Mercedes-Benz of Germany under which he secured the rights for Brazil. He secured 75% ownership for himself. He provided the capital. Last year Mercedes-Benz bought one third of his holdings for $14,000,000 to bring the two interests into 50–50 ownership. We walked through the plant with him; it is now producing six- and ten-ton trucks, all diesel, as well as great buses which use the same engine as the trucks.

The buses and trucks are sold on 24-month terms. I inferred that the corporation must insure the installment payments because Price said they had never lost "one cruzeiro" through bad credit or failure to pay.

The plant was clean and modern, only four years old, and a young man who was with us whispered to me, "the total capital on this plant was repaid by earnings in between 2 and 2½ years." (This represents the thinking of São Paulo capitalists, some of whom expect as much as 100% return a year on their money.) The engineer who showed us through the plant told us that Mercedes-Benz production today is 92% "national"–meaning that 92% of its materials are bought in Brazil. Within another year, he said, the production will be 99.5% national, with only 38 bearings imported from outside Brazil. Under a recent contract, Krupp has brought $20,000,000 worth of machinery into Brazil and is producing castings and forgings for Mercedes-Benz at a plant about 50 mi. away.

Of course, the dramatic fact brought home to me by this visit, coupled with my observation of the many plants in this new area, is the explosive nature of the São Paulo industrial development. Jurzykowski has made himself one of the world's richest men very quickly in Brazil.

KAISER INDUSTRIES CORP. in Córdoba, Argentina, known familiarly as I.K.A. (Industrias Kaiser Argentina), was the outstanding U.S.-created plant we visited. About 85% of all new cars sold in Argentina in 1959 came from this plant, the biggest single manufacturing enterprise in Argentina with a current annual volume of $100,000,000. Governor Stevenson and I were shown around the 1,600,000-sq. ft. plant by its manager, James McCloud, who told us its fascinating history.

After the failure of Kaiser-Frazer cars in the United States, Henry J. Kaiser, Sr., took his old dies and equipment from his Willow Run, Mich., plant and started up in Córdoba in 1955. One year later the plant was turning out cars. Thus far it has produced about 70,000 vehicles of various types—jeeps, tractors, station wagons, etc. More than 40,000 units of 15 different models were scheduled for 1960. McCloud told us that there is an unfilled Argentine demand for at least 1,000,000 vehicles. (He says that the average age of the cars on Argentine highways is between 15 and 20 years!) So, despite the fact that General Motors Corp., Ford Motor Co. and Chrysler Corp. are now opening plants in Argentina, McCloud hopes for a steadily rising production for Kaiser.

An important point is that, of the total outstanding stock of I.K.A., Argentine investors own 51% or more. Further, although McCloud started with 150 U.S. officers and employees, he has now replaced all but 32 of them with Argentines. I was told that I.K.A., including its Buenos Aires office for sales and finance, employs 6,000 people. (In my judgment the I.K.A. ownership pattern is sound: U.S. companies, if they wish to "export capitalism" and protect their investments in Latin America, would do well to extend to citizens of the countries where they operate a wider opportunity to acquire equity shares in their Latin-American subsidiaries and thus the opportunity to participate in earnings and dividends. This is one of the great issues of the future.)

The plant has a strong labor union with the men working 44 hours a week and being paid for 48. The average man on the line earns about $22 a week while men in the forge, doing more skilled and more dangerous work, earn about $26. This latter group had been trained by men sent down from Toledo, Ohio, during 1959. We saw them handling the hot metal with forceps and enormous "hammers," seemingly with great skill, and we were told that these men learned at least as fast as U.S. workmen. One of the Kaiser directors said that within a year he thought their productivity would actually exceed that of U.S. workmen; he said that they try harder and are more interested in their work.

Here is an outstanding example of U.S. enterprise and industry working in co-operation with Latin-American capital and labor. I cite it as well as the other examples to show how constructive and important the investment of foreign capital—and the importation of foreign business leadership—can be to the industrialization of these underdeveloped countries.

However, when I stress the value to Latin America of foreign investments in its industry, I do not mean to equate industrialization with such foreign capital. To Latin Americans the word industrialization does not primarily mean Anaconda Copper or Mercedes-Benz or the American & Foreign Power Company. It means Paz del Río, Colombia's steel-mill development; it means Huachipato, a similar development in Chile; and El Caroní, a combined electrification and metal-processing development in Venezuela. These latter symbolize the hope held by the Latin Americans themselves for their own industrial development; present governments may stand or fall on their success in stimulating such development. My emphasis on private foreign capital, here and in the paragraphs that follow, springs in part from the need for stressing its manifest importance and in part from the orientation of my visit, as set forth in my "Personal Preface"—the search for better understanding of Latin America by the people (and businessmen) of the United States—and for better understanding by their peoples of us. One grave difficulty faced in developing privately and locally owned industries in Latin

America is the lack of financial institutions which encourage the savings of small amounts and which thus accumulate large pools of capital. In the U.S.—through the life insurance companies, the building and loan associations and the mutual savings banks—some $200,000,000,000 of capital has been saved, mostly in small sums. This is roughly the value of our manufacturing plants. One of the greatest contributions to Latin-American economic development would be financial institutions which would encourage people to save small sums of money which would in turn be available to loan to industry. Recently Norman Bailey, an economist, wrote in the Columbia University *Forum* that the only way to develop a country's economy is through the formation of private capital. He writes, "The bureaucracies of the underdeveloped countries are inefficient always, and corrupt usually." He fears that public loans and grants from foreign countries will dampen internal effort and initiative. He points out that their total amount is bound to be very small—indeed, almost nothing—in contrast to the enormous needs. Although his view is an extreme one, it has many supporters and it does indeed help point up the necessity for capital formation by the Latin countries themselves.

More on the Role of Private Foreign Capital

As I have suggested, a U.S. economic policy towards Latin America that consists solely or primarily of a policy of encouraging private U.S. investment in Latin America is at best singularly inadequate. At the same time it is critically necessary to recognize the crucial role that private foreign capital has played and can play.

To anyone interested in the industrialization of Latin America, no truism is more obvious than this: Latin America is not going to realize any major part of its potential for economic development over the next decade without increased investment by private foreign investors as well as expanded credit from international lending agencies. Mexico appears to be the country most likely to advance under its own steam; 90% of Mexico's new investments since the end of World War II have come out of Mexico's own national income. But even Mexico seeks private foreign funds—although strictly on its own terms.[2]

More than $11,000,000,000 of United States money, public and private, is now invested in Latin America. The important fact which is least understood about this investment is that over 80% of it is private capital. Too few Latin Americans understand the value of these private contributions to their economies.

In 1957—the last year for which I could get figures—U.S. companies operating in Latin America produced more than $4,500,000,000 of goods and services for use in Latin America, and another $3,300,000,000 for export. They paid $7,000,000,000 for salaries, wages, taxes and purchase of local materials; of this, the $1,100,000,000 paid in taxes comprised approximately 20% of all the taxes paid in Latin America. They employed about 1,000,000 persons, only 2% of whom were from the U.S.

Over and over Governor Stevenson and I had to explain that, while it is appropriate for each country to lay down the broad terms of private foreign investment—and indeed through taxation to seek a share in its earnings, as most notably in the case of oil in Venezuela and copper in Chile—the central problem continues:

[2] Perhaps the best Mexican summation of "the outline and limitations of foreign investments," as he termed it, was provided for us by Antonio Ortiz Mena, Mexico's Minister of Finance. These were his eight points:

(1) Foreign investors in Mexico should scrupulously respect the laws and constitution of the host country and submit themselves in case of conflict to Mexican tribunals. (2) They should contribute to increasing the national income and, above all, to raising production in deficit areas. (3) They should stimulate foreign trade diversification and aim at equilibrium in the payments balance and at increasing the international financial capacity of the country. (4) They should not compete unfavourably with existing Mexican enterprises, or displace national capital or frustrate its future development. (5) They should renounce any political motive and contribute with all the means at their disposal to the creation of a favourable climate for economic development and industrialization. (6) They should introduce and employ advanced techniques to exploit productive resources more and more rationally, and thus improve the living conditions of the working population. (7) They should be directed to activities which provide impetus to and favour the integration of industrial development which reduces the dependency of the country on the production and export of raw materials and on the import of manufactures. (8) They should play a supplementary role in financing and in economic development.

this is to *attract* private capital. We had to point out again and again that private capital does not have to go to Latin America: it has many alternatives open to it within the United States, not to mention in other countries and continents. Indeed, one cause for present alarm is that there are some signs that Castro's expropriations may frighten away potential new private investments in other Latin countries. If so, this is cause for deep concern throughout the hemisphere.

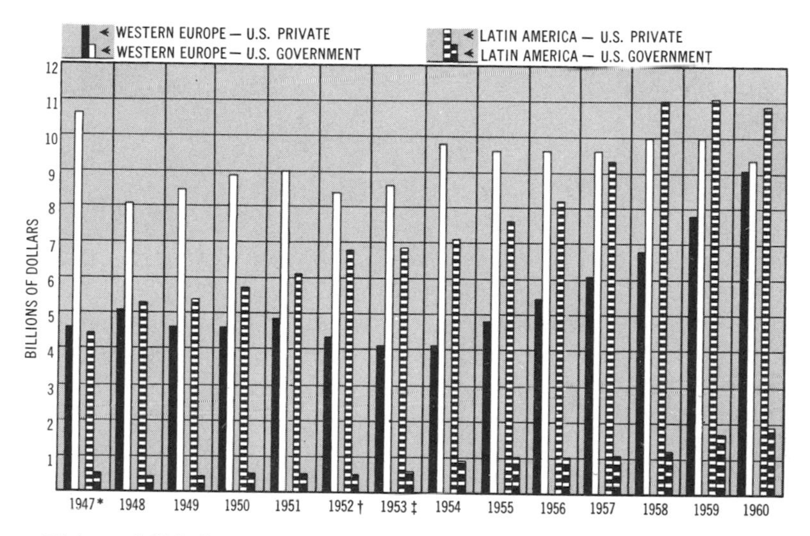

Value of U.S. investments, private and government, in Latin America and in western Europe, 1947–60. *European data 1947–51 are for all of Europe. †European data for 1952 include only Organization for European Economic Cooperation nations. ‡Data for 1953 are revised figures after a census of U. S. investments abroad. All data Dec.–Jan. or mid-year, as available. (*Source:* U.S. Department of Commerce)

International Basic Economy Corporation.—Even an investor as high-minded and as devoted to Latin America's welfare as Nelson Rockefeller must weigh alternatives. He may start a corporation to concentrate on Latin America but he will expand elsewhere if the rewards elsewhere are more promising. In 1947 Rockefeller and his brothers founded the International Basic Economy Corporation (IBEC). It seemed to them, to quote Governor Rockefeller's son Rodman, that "an American corporation could make a profit [in Latin America] by raising standards of living through exporting U.S. capital, management and technical knowledge into developing areas. Such a company could work with local investors in such basic fields as food and shelter to the benefit of everyone." The original investments in IBEC were about $17,000,000. They were all concentrated in Latin America. There were early mistakes, and for a time the investments seemed about to disappear.

"The company learned valuable lessons each time," says Rodman Rockefeller. "Consider, for example, IBEC's efforts to find the right combinations in Venezuela—the combinations that would bring profits by contributing to a better way of living. Investments in fishing and farming were unsuccessful, because of local conditions. A wholesale food distribution company was then set up to operate on a low-markup, high-volume basis, but retailers just kept their prices the same and took a bigger profit. That wasn't what IBEC wanted, so it studied new approaches. The one it came up with proved to be among its most successful ventures —the supermarket. When wholesaling failed, IBEC cracked the bottleneck by going into retailing.

IBEC opened Venezuela's first supermarket in 1949, with prices averaging 15% less than prevailing retail prices. Today there are 14 IBEC supermarkets in Venezuela, 5 of them in IBEC shopping centers. And IBEC itself in 1960 was operating in a dozen countries on four continents, in such diverse fields as housing, dairy products, food processing, mutual funds and trade financing. In other words, the opportunity for IBEC capital has proved tempting outside of Latin America as well as within; and the capital will flow where the opportunity beckons. This illustrates how the problem in each country is to attract the legitimate private capital in search of profits. IBEC sales are now running at $80,000,000 a year and its earnings at $2,200,000.

RESISTANCE AND SUSPICION.—The stake of U.S. private business in Latin America today is an imposing investment of $8,800,000,-000—four times the government loans. This figure, representing 35% of all direct U.S. private investment abroad, is larger than the figure for any other part of the world. Yet in many of the countries we visited the attitude towards U.S. private investment seemed to be one of resistance and suspicion—or at best of suspicious, grudging approval. This is not merely because of the lack of local participating capital. The other reasons for this attitude must be understood also if it is to be changed and if our private businesses are to continue—at an accelerated rate—to make the big contributions to the development of the Latin-American economy of which they are capable.

First and foremost may be the widespread belief that U.S. private business is "exploiting Latin America" through extortionate profits. At the Bogotá Economic Conference early in Sept. 1960 Cuba's Minister of Economy, Regino Boti, denouncing "North American imperialistic capitalism," estimated U.S. investments in Latin America at $10,000,000,000, and placed the annual earnings on this investment at $1,500,000,000. He urged other Latin-American countries to finance their industrialization through "forced loans" from U.S. companies. Boti's figures are erroneous. The profits on the average are not excessive. Further, when account is taken of U.S. private earnings reinvested in Latin America, and of the annual flow of fresh U.S. dollar investments, the net flow of dollars back to the U.S. from private investment in Latin America probably does not exceed 2% and is perhaps closer to 1%.

Venezuela's Foreign Minister, Ignacio Luis Arcaya Rivero, since resigned, described other kinds of suspicions many Latin Americans hold toward U.S. big business. Many feel the power of the U.S. government is primarily aimed to strengthen and entrench the position of our corporations. Many claim, he said, that when Latin-American countries seek technical assistance the United States seeks always to tie this into investments by U.S. privately controlled corporations. When Latin America wants loans for government projects, he went on, the U.S. again talks about private enterprise. He repeated—with emphasis—"This point is very important!" (Another leading Venezuelan politician had commented that Pres. Dwight Eisenhower's speeches in his early 1960 tour of Latin America "were those of a traveling salesman for American business," and repeatedly we were told, "The cornerstone of U.S. policy isn't so much to make Latin America safe for democracy as it is to make it safe for American private corporations.")

Arcaya Rivero did indeed compliment highly the sense of public responsibility of our businessmen—but with a warning. He stressed the point that Latin-American millionaires and businessmen were of a very different breed from those in the United States. The Latin-American distrust of U.S. private investors, he implied, springs in part from their distrust of their own rich in-

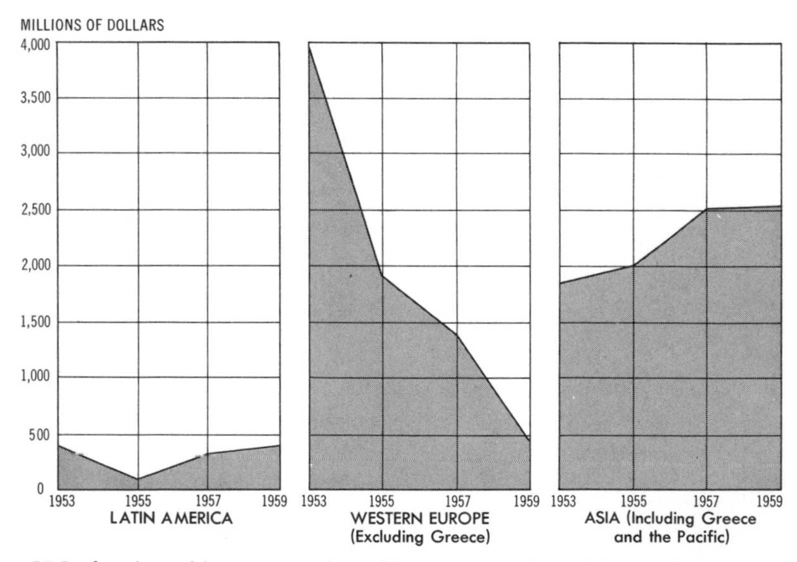

U.S. foreign aid grants and credits to countries of Latin America, western Europe and Asia, 1953–59. (*Source:* Statistical Abstract of the United States, 1960)

vestors. U.S. businessmen, he said, "have traditions of public service"; they have developed a "sense of public trust." Then he emphasized, "This sense of public service is unknown among Latin-American businessmen." To illustrate his point, the minister told us that the town where President Betancourt of Venezuela was born has three or four rich families, but the town has no roads, no schools. The rich families, he says, are wholly indifferent to these needs.

This difference in attitude, according to the minister, "is a major point which you in the U.S. must understand if you are to comprehend misunderstandings in Latin America about U.S. businessmen and big business. He said he understood it because he had lived five years in exile in the U.S. and indeed, if the Latin Americans mistrust their own rich, it does seem natural for many of them to view our big corporations similarly.

Most U.S. firms operating in Latin America carry south with them the standards they have developed—and have often been required by regulations to develop—at home. These standards include maintaining a single set of books, bringing in outside auditors, publishing financial reports, paying full taxes, complying with local labor laws and trying to avoid bribery. Their example is not always appreciated by local Latin-American businessmen. This too has been a source of criticism, and thus our corporations have been attacked from the right as well as the left.

Frank Tannenbaum gives further insight into the Latin dislike of U.S. business and investors. With understanding of Latin culture, he writes:[3]

> This Latin American objection to American enterprise is not that it is American. Rather it is disliked because it is efficient, purposeful, direct, singleminded and materialistic. In Latin American culture, business is part of the total scheme of things; it is part of the family, of the *compadre* relation, of the friendships, of the Church. It is done among friends in a leisurely and understanding way—the efficiency and singlemindedness of the American enter-

[3] In *The United States and Latin America*, American Assembly of Columbia University, December 1959.

> prise is unaware of and indifferent to the scheme of ethical and aesthetic values by which life is ruled. Its very egalitarianism and familiarity are offensive—and Americans are not particularly helpful in this. They do not, for the most part, associate with the members of their host community, and if they have to, they often do it in a patronizing way.

Time after time I heard the same theme reiterated—that Latin-American businessmen and landowners have less social consciousness, that they take little part in welfare activities, that they seldom contribute to education, that they duck their fair share of the burden of taxation. In short, they sound much like some of our predatory businessmen who grew rich in the 19th-century United States. One foreign minister told me, "Your American businessmen changed their spots; perhaps we can hope that ours will too."

U.S. SHORTCOMINGS.—Yet there is much more to the story, on which I shall only touch. There are items on the debit side of the double-entry ledger. Our businessmen both in the U.S. and abroad have often engaged in monopoly practices which do indeed exploit the customers; they have frequently, even if unconsciously, unfairly held down wages and fought the development of free unions; they have held back education, opposed the development of welfare practices, demanded a type of so-called "free economy" which for a generation has been unknown in the U.S. Here is how we look to James Morris in an article on Cuba published in the *New York Times* magazine section on August 7, 1960. There many of our businessmen, as well as our gangsters, were affiliated with the Batista dictatorship. In Cuba, the imprint of the U.S. was at its worst.

Morris is no Cuban revolutionary. He is the correspondent of the *Manchester Guardian*. He wrote from Havana:

> The United States' presence in the Caribbean is not, to European eyes, an agreeable spectacle. Its undertones (whether real or imaginary) of monopoly, cartel exploitation and exclusivity strike harshly upon the old-fashioned imperial mind, accustomed to the notion of duty as a prerequisite of dominion.
>
> The contrast the United States has fostered between vulgar af-

fluence and ignorant poverty, only a couple of hundred miles from the dear old ladies of Tampa and St. Petersburg, is ugly to contemplate. Its alliances with flashy dictators, crooked promoters, pimps and fly-by-nighters seem terribly unworthy of the world's prime liberty men. It has smeared across these heavenly seas and idyllic islands a veneer of heartless profit, unwholesome tourism, cheap materialism and all these rituals of the American Way which, thus transplanted from their rustic breeding grounds, do so much to tarnish the image of the Law, the one common denominator of decent peoples. . . .

U.S. Contributions.—Despite criticisms of this kind, and despite the legitimate fears they have on other counts, I believe it is fair to say that most Latin Americans welcome United States and other foreign private investors, most especially when they supply know-how and leadership as well as capital. They are most welcome in the more progressive and dynamic societies. They are even more welcome when they do not represent the power of our colossal supercorporations like Standard Oil. Costa Rica's José Figueres told me about a U.S. GI who came to Costa Rica after the war and developed a new chicken industry—"a whole new industry, revolutionizing the raising of chickens here; his leadership and skill were far more important than his $10,000 capital."

Figueres told me also about a young U.S. pilot named Robert Anson who came to Costa Rica after the war and founded a company to fix airplanes. The company, named SALA, now employs 400 Costa Ricans and only two Americans. Planes come to SALA from as far away as Canada and Argentina to get complete technical and mechanical overhauling. This story, said Figueres, shows what Costa Rica needs over and above capital. It may also be an example of the opportunity awaiting young and talented men who can bring leadership and know-how in certain key fields to Latin America.

United States Government Investment and Technical Aid

Of course, low interest loans to Latin-American governments from U.S. governmental or international agencies are also urgently needed. At the time of our visit, Latin America had such current outstanding loans of $2,300,000,000.[4] With the help of such loans, Latin-American governments are increasingly involved in industrial production; approximately 25% of the gross industrial product of the entire region comes from publicly owned enterprises.

However, all such loans do not go into enterprises owned or operated by governments. At a formal lunch in Santiago, Chile, I sat next to Don Eduardo Figueroa, president of the Banco Central of Chile, a short, good-looking man who is one of South America's most eligible bachelors. He had previously been in charge of the new steel mill in Concepción that was financed by the Export-Import bank. He had spent five years at M.I.T., in Pittsburgh and

[4] Of this amount the Export-Import bank, an agency of the United States government, had loaned by far the largest share—$1,314,000,000 presently outstanding. Principal borrowers from the Export-Import bank were six countries which had together absorbed almost 90% of the credits. Brazil alone accounted for 38%, Argentina, 16% and Mexico, 12%.

The International Bank for Reconstruction and Development, commonly called the World bank, had outstanding loans in Latin America of $590,000,000, of which Brazil had received 29%, Mexico, 21% and Colombia, 12%. The International Monetary fund had loaned a total of $333,000,000, of which the principal recipients were Brazil, with $85,000,000, Chile, $55,000,000 and Argentina, $75,000,000. Still another institution providing capital for economic development is the Development Loan fund, from which, as of January 1959, Latin America had received $50,000,000.

Under U.S. public law 480, Latin-American countries can get further resources for economic development from their purchases of United States surplus agricultural commodities. As of January 1, 1959, Latin America had absorbed $350,000,000 of this surplus since the program's inception in 1954. The local currencies which they pay for these commodities belong to the United States, but about 85% of them have been lent to the respective governments to help finance various local development projects.

The final source from which Latin-American countries are now able to obtain publicly supplied capital is the new Inter-American Development bank, organized in 1959. This bank is capitalized at $1,000,000,000, of which $150.000,000 is to be used as a Fund for Special Operations, or so-called "soft" loans, while the other $850,000,000 is for hard currency loans. Too new to have had any appreciable effect on the Latin economy as yet, this bank can, in time, increase measurably the public capital constructively invested in Latin America.

NOTE: The foregoing figures are given by Reynold E. Carlson of Vanderbilt University in his chapter in *The United States and Latin America* published by the American Assembly of Columbia University, December 1959.

elsewhere in the U.S., preparing for this job. Figueroa told me that the financing cost of the mill was $140,000,000, of which the Export-Import bank put up $80,000,000, which is being repaid. The Chilean government guaranteed the loan and put up the other $60,000,000, then sold part of the equity to Chilean private citizens who operate the mill. This last is an important point.

Present production is about 450,000 ingots, of which 75% is used domestically and the rest exported. Figueroa said that the base cost of producing the "hot steel" is as low as it is in the United States, but the total cost averages 25%–30% higher because there is not yet sufficient production against which to distribute overhead and financial costs. With double the present production, he said over-all costs will equal those in Gary, Ind.

Mr. Figueroa stressed the fact that the $80,000,000 borrowed from the Export-Import bank was all spent in the United States. He said it was divided among a large number of suppliers and thus created considerable business for us. He told me also that the 135 U.S. families who lived in Concepción during the mill's construction "did very great good to achieving understanding of North Americans." He was obviously proud of this example of United States co-operation in Chile's industrialization.

This story again illustrates the point that there may be too much concentration on the need for foreign capital, which is obvious, and not enough talk about the need for the 135 families and the kind of know-how which comes with them. Because of inadequate, old-fashioned educational facilities in Latin America—which I will discuss at length in a separate section—there is in Latin America a great shortage of personnel trained in modern agricultural and industrial methods. Though both capital and technical skill are needed, efficient use of the world's most advanced techniques can contribute enormously to the productivity of capital in spurring the development of the Latin economy. Through the contribution of both, we of the U.S. can best help the Latin Americans help themselves.

This brings me to our government's program of technical assistance for Latin America. The first such significant program was the one developed before our entry into World War II by Nelson Rockefeller's Office of Inter-American Affairs, which I later inherited when I became Assistant Secretary of State. When the same concept was applied by Pres. Harry S. Truman to underdeveloped countries everywhere, it became known as Point Four. It is an ideal way for the U.S. to help underdeveloped nations, for ideally, it is aimed at helping such countries through cultivation and development of their own knowledge and brain power. In the long run this is the least expensive help we can give and also the most effective per dollar.

During the years 1946–1959 the U.S. government gave total financial assistance to Latin-American governments in the form of grants and loans of $3,840,000,000. Of this only $203,700,000 was for technical co-operation. In fiscal 1959, for example, $34,-300,000 was earmarked for such technical assistance. This covers all Point Four projects. All of them are joint enterprises between the U.S. and the co-operating countries. In 1959 Latin-American financial contributions to these projects far exceeded in total the U.S. contributions; indeed, many projects initiated by U.S. officials have been taken over entirely by their Latin-American hosts.

Point Four programs are essentially demonstration projects. They are administered in Washington by the International Co-operation Administration and in the field by "operations missions" attached to each U.S. embassy. Latin-American activities are carried out chiefly through 47 *servicios* in 17 countries—centers maintained jointly by the U.S. operations missions and the host governments. In 1959 these *servicios* employed more than 19,000 Latin Americans on in-service training projects. In addition, 12 U.S. universities had contracts for special projects. Several hundred U.S. experts were in Latin America at any one time, and in 1959 about 2,000 Latin Americans were sent to the U.S. and other countries for training.

Originally these technical co-operation projects focused on agriculture, education and public health. In agriculture, modern methods of crop diversification were taught, and youth groups comparable to our 4-H clubs were organized. More recently the scope of these projects has been widened to include industry, mining, transportation, housing, communications and public administration. For example, the University of Tennessee undertook training for public administration in Bolivia and Panamá.

Here in such a program we have an example of enlightened U.S. economic policy at its best; and here we have also the kinds of projects which add to the productivity of foreign capital investment.

Inflation—the Devourer

Since World War II one of Latin America's chronic and acute economic headaches has been inflation. The evil impact of inflation is too well known for me to belabor here. In amount, it has varied from country to country but has been particularly severe in Argentina, Brazil, Paraguay, Bolivia, Uruguay and Chile. Since 1953 the cost-of-living index for Uruguay rose 244%, for Argentina 464%, for Brazil 326%, for Paraguay 240%, for Chile 1,043% and for Bolivia 3,005%. Under an agreement with the International Monetary fund and the treasury of the United States, these countries, with one exception, in 1960 were pursuing programs of "austerity" designed to check inflation. As this article went to press, there were many hopeful signs.

CHILE is one of the countries making a determined effort to curb inflation. Over the period 1940–1955 Chile experienced a 1,600% inflation. For the year 1956 the rate of inflation was 85%; for 1957, 40%. In 1958 the rate was cut to 20%, but in 1959 it was back up to 45%. The higher-income groups in general have been able to dance ahead of this inflation, and by and large the middle groups have held their own. But the lower-income Chileans have steadily lost out. Food now takes 60% to 80% of a Chilean laborer's pay.

Chile's President Alessandri told us that he is now trying to correct the imbalance between local and world prices. He explained that "we are now at the most difficult point; we've had 20 years of demagogic government; the salaried classes expect automatic increases and this gives away the productive capacity of the country faster than we can increase it." He said he was faced with a "big opposition campaign." Last year such a campaign forced him "to raise salaries and wages 30%." This year the same increase is demanded once more. He is against it.

He told us the story of the Schweiger Coal company, which has an annual profit of $160,000. An increase in wages of 10% would create an extra expense of $480,000. The opposition has demanded a 35% increase. To cover this increase, the price of coal would have to go up. The president added, "I have ordered that there shall be no rise in coal prices. Of course, the Schweiger Coal company can raise wages if it wishes!" (A U.S. expert on labor with whom I talked said he had visited the Schweiger Coal company and found that its output per worker was one-eighth that of U.S. mines because of antiquated machinery and methods. It probably cannot get far enough ahead of the game to modernize. The expert said, "No wonder the annual profit of the Schweiger Coal company was only $160,000!")

ARGENTINA, suffering from the disastrous fiscal policies of Juan Perón, is also struggling to counteract inflation and revert to a sound economic base. Argentina has little unemployment. Alsogaray, the minister of the economy appointed by President Frondizi in June 1959, told us that his big job is to persuade the people of Argentina to support his financial retrenchment policies actively. Central to his objective is a campaign to hold down prices.

Minister Alsogaray, an aggressive and dynamic man with conservative ideas, conceded that the Argentine economy had suffered in recent months from strikes and other difficulties. However, he felt that "today things are going well—except for small acts of terrorism." He said the people were beginning to realize that his way is "the only way." The local elections in Argentina after we left, in which President Frondizi's party came in third, were not encouraging to his cause.

BRAZIL.—The one great exception to "austerity" as a curb to inflation, of course, has been Brazil, which has suffered one of the greatest inflations in recent times, averaging over 50% a year.

But other things have seemed more important to Brazil's leaders, and throughout the Kubitschek administration no one of influence seemed to have the faintest intention of turning to austerity in an effort to stop the inflation—or to have any other idea of how to stop it—least of all President Kubitschek.

A Brazilian businessman told me something of how inflation is working within the Brazilian economy. He described two kinds of inflation operating in Brazil. Both depend on printing-press money but one pushes up prices more rapidly than the other. The first was the printing of money for the running expenses of government. For example, while we were in Rio, then President Kubitschek ordered the finance minister to print more money to pay the increases in salaries for government employees. This only rated a small item on page two of the local English-language newspaper. Everyone is used to this by now. The second kind was what my friend termed "hot money." For example, the minute the farmers get the cash for their coffee, they rush out to buy almost anything into which they can convert it because they know that their money is going to depreciate in value. This, of course, forces prices up still faster. My business acquaintance felt that President Kubitschek made the wrong decision in 1959 in paying the coffee growers cash for their crop; he felt that they should have been paid in treasury notes payable over a period of time. But of course great political pressure was on the President to dole out the quick cash, in part because of the inflation, and this of course involved running the printing presses.

This businessman estimated that the current inflation in Brazil is roughly comparable to a 10% or 15% extra tax on the workers. The rise in wages and salaries always lags a good 10% or 15% behind the rise in prices. I found this a most important observation. It helps explain how Brazil's extreme inflation is helping to finance its boom economy and why so many rich people, including bankers and industrialists, do not resist it. They have learned to ride up with it in their profits and capital. Governor Stevenson and I marveled at the way bankers and industrialists in Brazil rationalize the inflation. The labor groups are of course opposed to it. This is roughly opposite to the way the counterparts of these groups line up in the United States. In our country, the conservative groups press aggressively for a balanced budget and a stable price system, while labor tends to favor a so-called "easy money" policy, even at the risk of some inflation.

In the Federal District of Brazil the minimum wage in 1956 was 3,800 cruzeiros a month. In 1959 it was 6,000. But real wages declined far more than this because of price rises. Reynold Carlson of Vanderbilt University says of this: "Using the free market exchange rate for a rough approximation, the monthly minimum wage in 1956 was equivalent to $57.50, whereas the 1959 rate was equivalent to $44.50." Many businessmen have learned how to profit by these deteriorating wages.

The Brazilian inflation has also hurt sharply all groups dependent on fixed incomes, and it has decimated the value of life insurance. This has created terrible injustices. Carlson believes Brazil's recent spotty but phenomenal growth has been achieved in spite of inflation and not because of it.

Inflation pulls society apart, creates monstrous political problems, promotes extremist politics and turns some businessmen into opportunistic wolves. But in its peculiar and unfortunate way it can, temporarily at least, contribute to capital growth. One way a man with money can keep up with its depreciation is through capital investments which appreciate.

I listened to a group of businessmen in São Paulo one day trying to figure out what to do with $1,000,000 to preserve its purchasing power five years hence. They arbitrarily assumed something they could not know for sure: that money would continue to depreciate at no more than 50% a year. Not one of these men had any certain answer. All agreed that one major possibility is for the money to seek capital assets which will appreciate faster than money depreciates. This is not easy because of political and other risks.

The fever of an inflationary boom has infected the Brazilian economy for 20 years. Although its cost has been frightful to many groups, one rule has generally been followed by businessmen who have not wanted to indulge in constant and continuous speculation and gambling. The rule is to keep the money in one's own business and to "keep turning it over as fast as possible." On this basis some businesses claim they earn 100% a year or more on their capital. This of course may not amount to a true 100% with capital depreciating by 50%. But obviously many are earning vast fortunes. In an inflation, there are always men clever enough to capitalize on it—particularly in such a country as Brazil with vast commercial potential. There are many men in São Paulo with incomes running into many millions of dollars a year.

Brazil has long thought of itself as being one of the best friends of the United States in the southern hemisphere. But today there is tension between our countries, particularly on economic issues. As a result of the inflationary policies of the Brazilian government the United States has not looked favorably on granting further major loans to Brazil. Certain Brazilians have resented this attitude.

Between the conclusion of our trip and the time this is being written, Brazil has installed a new president, and its monetary and fiscal policies may change. The results of the efforts of the Chileans, the Argentines and others to curb their inflations remain to be seen, as do the hazards and penalties of recent Brazilian policy.

World Commodity Prices and Latin America's Exports

Many of the countries of Latin America depend for foreign exchange on one or two export products, such as coffee or copper. Their economic health fluctuates with the going prices of the commodities. Fluctuations in the world prices of such basic commodities as ores, sugar, cocoa and coffee may be as great as 25%–50% in a year, and of course bulk sales volume fluctuates as well. Yet revenue from these exports and the tax yield from the exporting companies support not only the purchase of imports but also in an important degree the operations of the governments of many countries. For example, a change of one cent a pound in the world price of copper means $7,000,000 a year to the treasury of

Chile. The drop in world coffee prices from 60 cents to 40 cents a pound over the past decade is estimated to have cost Latin America $1,000,000,000.

Fourteen of the 20 republics depend on a single commodity for one half or more of all their export earnings; ten of these get 75% of their earnings from two top exports. Because the United States is their biggest market, many Latin Americans blame the United States when prices are low. (We were even told that it is "well known" that coffee prices are set in New York.)

The problem is intensified because competition in world markets against Latin America's primary products is increasing, notably from Asia and Africa. Synthetics—even for coffee—threaten Latin-American commodity exports.

Everywhere we went anxious voices asked whether and how world markets and prices could be stabilized. This is an exceedingly difficult problem, in part because U.S. policy is committed to free markets. It is difficult because ordinarily we have felt unable to control world prices even if we had wanted to.

Labor Unions

Of course it is in the labor forces of the big U.S. corporations operating in Latin America that the politically oriented labor unions tend to be most active. It is here that the Communist operatives try to stir up real or fancied grievances. Thus they concentrate on such unions as those of the United Fruit Co. in Costa Rica, Cuba, Ecuador, Guatemala and Honduras—and those of the petroleum workers in Venezuela. Yet many U.S. firms seem to be able to provide the leadership, direction and incentives that make the men want to work without strikes or undue agitation. In Mendoza, Argentina, we had heard the complaint that farm hands were not doing their work in the vineyards—that they would work for three or four days and, when they had a little money for food and wine, they would quit. This complaint did not apply to the workmen for U.S. firms such as I.K.A. in Córdoba, which has a waiting list for jobs of about 30,000 persons. Indeed, as I pointed out a moment ago, the attacks on the labor relations of U.S. corporations may come from the right rather than the left. I was told by one U.S. ambassador that many U.S. firms in Latin America are criticized by native businessmen because they pay their workers better, because they seek to keep their wages abreast of the rising cost of living, because they give their workers fringe benefits and help them become better educated.

In no country we visited did we find labor as strong and stable as its U.S. counterpart. With few exceptions there are no strong national unions. Many of the unions belong to the Organización Regional Interamericana de Trabajadores (ORIT), which a Colombian labor leader told me was almost singlehandedly created by Serafino Romualdi, the able and famous inter-American representative of the AFL-CIO. ORIT was set up as the western hemisphere branch subsidiary of the world-wide International Confederation of Free Trade Unions (ICFTU). An important goal is to combat Communist penetration of the labor movement in Latin America. ORIT has a number of seminars each year, and we were told by Romualdi that ORIT's director of education is an American and that his program is "quite successful." He tries to fight "fascist dictatorships" as well as Communist infiltration. At the same time ORIT's department of organization, headed by a Peruvian, is helping to organize free unions.

Labor and Politics.—With ORIT's encouragement, hundreds of Latin labor leaders—300 to 400 a year—come to the United States under Point Four. Conversely, a number of our labor union leaders have visited the Latin countries. The leaders of North and South America co-operate in many ways. In Mexico there is a Samuel Gompers Club, with monthly lectures; in Chile, there is an Abraham Lincoln Club. In most Latin-American countries the labor unions have been politically lined up against dictators—but in Cuba most of the leaders of the labor movement made a deal with Batista and supported him. Romualdi said that the Cuban leaders were trying to disengage themselves when Batista fell. Castro's new labor leaders have refused to co-operate with the

AFL-CIO. This followed their decision to disaffiliate from the ORIT-ICFTU, taken at the November 1959 Cuban labor convention, when the Communists gained control.

Romualdi told us that as a political force Latin-American labor unions are getting more independent politically, and thus stronger. In Mexico the biggest labor union has been part and parcel of the government party. Because it has had no real independence, there is a great deal of discontent with its leadership. We were told that in the not too distant future, Mexican labor may try to break away from the government and seek to develop financial and trade-union independence.

Many Latin-American countries have adopted elaborate social welfare legislation. In many cases they have copied the legislation of far more advanced countries. (However, Uruguay and Chile were world pioneers in some types of social security.) The cost of these benefits has been a heavy addition to the wage bill and in most cases has not been balanced by increases in productivity. In Uruguay "social welfare" is said to account in some occupations for as much as 25% of the total payroll, and the "take" is also heavy in Brazil and Argentina. In Argentina and Uruguay the workers in several occupations can retire at 55 with a pension of almost 100% of salary. Railway workers in Argentina struck recently, demanding 86% on retirement. We are told that this demand was not fomented by organized labor as much as by the politicians. The latter seek the short-run benefits of labor union tie-ups in terms of votes. The dilemma for the laborer has been that as savings or pension funds accrue, inflation has eaten them up and the workers have been no better off and often worse off because of their dependence on the politicians.

The labor unions of Brazil are an example of those that have been government controlled. During his dictatorship, Vargas saw to it that they were run entirely by the government. And even today a union cannot be started in Brazil without a government permit. In theory, the Brazilian government decides all important wage matters. In theory, too, strikes are illegal. In practice they are beginning to occur with increasing frequency. In the state of

São Paulo alone there were about 300 strikes in 1959, most of them caused by worker discontent with the inflationary spiral in the cost of living.

Under the Brazilian system, the government collects all the dues and keeps about 20% for so-called "educational and recreational purposes." With the 20%, the government can maintain several hundred sinecures to bestow at its own discretion on labor leaders who do its bidding. In this way the government possesses both a big carrot and a big stick. Some observers think this arrangement should keep government in control of the labor unions for many years. Others report that many Brazilian labor leaders are increasingly restless under government domination and want independence.

In Bogotá the leader of a Colombian petroleum union, Luis Alfonso Perdomo, suggested that Governor Stevenson and I call upon U.S. businessmen in Latin America to show much greater understanding of the problems of the workers. He told us that the United States has been hurt by the seeming alliance of our business leaders with Latin-American dictators who oppress the workers, and he referred to a "McCarthyesque attitude" on the part of our businessmen overseas. He said that they often joined hands with the dictators to label efforts by labor unions for social progress as "a socialist plot." I asked him if he didn't feel that U.S. business had indeed improved in its attitudes. He agreed that it had—"since May 10, 1957, when the Rojas dictatorship fell!" (in Colombia).

To summarize: A major weakness in the Latin-American economy (and in Latin-American politics) is the weakness of the labor unions. Many are Communist controlled and many more are politically oriented. One of the great hopes for the strengthening of the Latin-American economies is the development of strong unions free of political domination. This hope is linked with the elimination of illiteracy and the improvement of education. Toward this goal, the International Confederation of Free Trade Unions, the International Federation of Christian Trade Unions and the AFL-CIO can make an even greater contribution.

The Common Market

I have been emphasizing Latin-American economic problems—as problems. There are also elements of promise. One is the hoped-for development of a "common market" for the region as a whole.

One brake to the economic progress of Latin America has been the pitifully small amount of trade among the Latin-American countries themselves; only about 10% of the total foreign trade of the 20 republics is within Latin America. This has not only been due to the natural geographic obstacles, and the lack of adequate roads and transportation, referred to in the opening section. It is also due to the fact that principal exports have been competitive rather than complementary, and to the stubborn regionalistic feelings that have had a tendency to keep one Latin-American country from doing business with another. Then, of course, there has been the skill of Europe and the U.S. in developing two-way trade. I was even told that the United States, by not actively promoting a common market, had been chiefly responsible for its failure to develop. And I do indeed agree that we have dragged our feet; we have failed to provide sufficient encouragement toward such a goal. Perhaps this is not unnatural; it is the traditional diplomatic attitude of *divide et impera.*

The first steps toward a common market in Latin America were taken in 1960. Argentina, Brazil, Chile, Mexico, Paraguay, Peru and Uruguay signed a treaty linking a portion of their economies. This took place just as Governor Stevenson and I started our trip. Bolivia was expected to join the pact shortly. Agriculture and livestock—the most important items of the countries' economies—are specifically excluded. Yet the agreement should provide a foundation for more efficient economic development and for more rapid industrialization. At about the same time, agreements were drawn up envisaging a similar common market arrangement among several Central American nations, specifically El Salvador, Guatemala, Honduras and Nicaragua. It was believed that Costa Rica and Panamá would also join.

If the U.S. takes the statesmanlike view now called for by

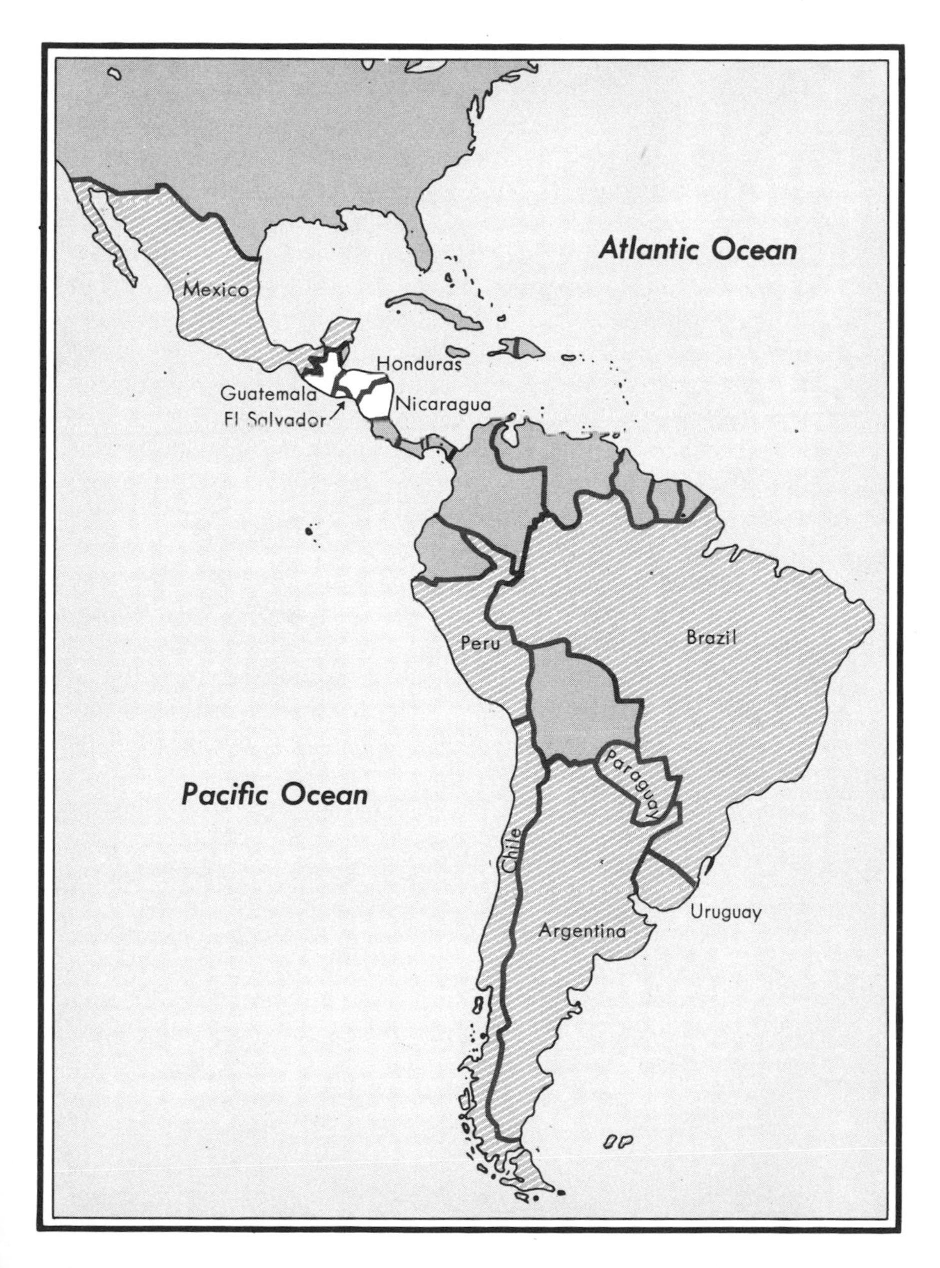

Two areas of common markets which were being planned in 1960. Bolivia was expected to join the one with Mexico and the South American countries; Costa Rica and Panama were likely members of the other group.

the world crisis, we should applaud these developments and encourage their expansion and implementation. We should gladly concede that, in the long run, what is good for the Latin-American economy should be good for the United States. Indeed, a Latin-American common market, or two of them, will develop the entire region into a bigger and better market for our goods. More importantly, such arrangements will help Latin America stand firmly on its own economic feet. It will thus need less help from us.

This latter is indeed urgently to be desired if only because the Latin leaders in general tend to expect a great deal more help from the United States than we can possibly give. Even the $600,000,000 President Eisenhower mentioned in July, 1960, during one of our recurrent Cuban crises will not seem large to them. With some notable exceptions they either overlook or fail to understand the nature of our present world responsibilities—our obligations in Asia, Europe and elsewhere—and why it is important to them that we continue to shoulder such responsibilities. For the long run, of course, they will agree that they would prefer not to be dependent on the U.S. The common market is one approach toward reducing that dependence.

Operation "Pan America"

Even before the establishment of the republic in Brazil in 1891 Brazilians aspired to a special relationship with the United States, and on a bilateral basis. Brazil has long felt it was destined to be the great power in the south, as is the United States in the north.

The dream of partnership has faded. The United States in recent years has sought to work out hemispheric problems increasingly on a multilateral basis, most recently through the Organization of American States which includes all the American republics.

In an attempt to assert Brazil's claim to leadership in South America, and to exert pressure on the United States, former President Kubitschek publicized a program which he called "Operation Pan America," or OPA. This was a bid for big-time financial backing for Latin America by the U.S. It was more than this, but it was this in the first place. Acting as world ambassador on behalf of President Kubitschek's plan was a wealthy Brazilian businessman with a chain of supermarkets and a reputation as a poet, Augusto Frederico Schmidt. Schmidt was a close personal associate of the president and is said to have written some of the president's statements.

Schmidt called upon us in Rio and explained that the idea for OPA "flowed from an act of friendship by Brazil toward the United States after the attacks on Vice-President Nixon in Lima and Caracas in 1958." He added that President Kubitschek had personally wanted "to do something about the anti-American feeling." "OPA does not mean forming any new organization," he insisted. "We do not want to create more diplomatic jobs that will accomplish nothing."

As a political policy, OPA was an effective slogan for President Kubitschek. Neither he nor Schmidt wanted to spell it out in terms of financial commitments from the United States. They preferred keeping the ball in our court. (Castro is increasingly making this a ball which we must return as a golden ball.) Schmidt told us that U.S.-Brazilian economic relations were deteriorating. He reported that German trade and prestige in Brazil were growing. A number of Brazilian industries, he warned us, are now being financed by Europeans.

Having heard about the rapid growth of Polish trade in Brazil, I asked Schmidt about this. He replied that the Poles give credits on steel and machinery that "no American would ever dream of." Schmidt told us that he was about to become Brazilian ambassador to Europe's Common Market, where he would "explain the OPA to Europe" and develop Brazil's European trade. Why doesn't the United States Government, he asked, help U.S. firms who want to extend credits to Brazil?

Schmidt told us he was struggling to develop an economic plan for Latin America. He wanted a plan that was "an instrument of reason." He suggested that the Inter-American bank bring new techniques to Latin America. He urged, "Let it help educate Latin America for the new age."

Although I am sure Schmidt was familiar with U.S. economic aid to Brazil, throughout our meeting there was no mention of the extensive program of technical co-operation which the United States has maintained in Brazil which since the start of the bilateral programs in 1943 has exceeded $50,000,000 in cost. Nor did he accord any recognition of the $8,000,000 being spent to eradicate malaria in Brazil, or of similar programs. Obviously he wanted much more.

The propaganda implications in OPA were shown in an advertisement signed by President Kubitschek and published in the *New York Times* on August 2, 1960. This was the text of a letter he had sent to President Eisenhower. This was a riposte to President Eisenhower's announcement in July of the great new financial program of loans and grants for Latin America. (The timing of this announcement made many Latins believe that Castro was to be thanked for Uncle Sam's sudden new generosity.) This advertisement read in part:

> Permit me to reaffirm to Your Excellency what already has been said concerning Operation Pan America: It is not a question of an appeal to generosity, but to reason. Reason dictates the necessity of fighting in the only efficacious manner against the cold war which insinuates itself and seeks to involve our Continent. The fight which all of us must undertake together for the common ideals of the Americas will be valid only if we combat the causes of unrest and discontent, without seeking merely to correct and diminish their effects and consequences.
>
> We ought, therefore, to have the courage to draw the conclusions which reality presents to us. The truth is that, despite all previous efforts, not enough has been done and an adequate rate of development for the Latin American peoples has not been achieved. To wish to attribute the present unrest of these peoples to mere propaganda or agitation by extra-continental agents would be to ignore the fact that poverty and the frustration of economically stagnant peoples have a much greater capability for agitation. The problem therefore consists in giving a new dimension to the work to be accomplished. . . .

The Brazilian President called for "a more active collaboration in our development through a new policy of public financing, in which would be observed other criteria than that of mere immediate profitability."

Ambassador E. P. Barbosa da Silva, former head of the Economic Department of the Ministry of Foreign Affairs, described OPA as "the bringing together of twenty-one peoples in a common effort to promote and safeguard moral and spiritual values received as a common legacy by means of a concerted action against poverty and ignorance. . . ." Through OPA Pan Americanism would carry a new message and an inspiration. Its success would have a tremendous impact in Africa and in Southeast Asia. Its failure would reveal the unquestionable defeat of democratic ideals in the less developed world—democracy would be doomed."

OPA is not a planning group nor does it seek to create one. It is skillful political action to put ever greater pressure on the United States. And why not? There will be more Kubitscheks and more OPA's as there will be more Castros. We must expect them. And often it will be the better part of statesmanship not to throw up our arms in immediate and automatic resistance to them.

In Conclusion, Three Highlights on Economic Problems

In reviewing this long section dealing with some of the economic problems and needs in Latin America, three highlights of my impressions should perhaps be stressed:

Mushrooming new industries are absorbing more and more workers whose living standards do not rise as they should—in part because inflation negates their gains.

A steady growth of the total labor force, stimulated by the surging population increase and abetted by the rush to the cities, is resulting in increased unemployment and the threat of still more. In the rural areas, the land and the agricultural techniques are inadequate. In the cities the economic problem becomes an acute social and human problem. The next decade must bring far greater realization of the hopes of the submerged half of the population. If it does not, I fear that the free world will suffer a series of damaging blows.

Despite—or perhaps because of—over-all economic gains, there is a growing yearning and demand for human dignity on a far broader scale. This demand too must be met. If it is not, the United States and the free world are in danger.

3

The Threatening Cloud—Communism Plus Castroism

In the country of our second stop José Figueres, Costa Rica's former President, told Governor Stevenson and me of his deep concern about Communist influence in Latin America. Throughout our trip, most of the responsible leaders, both liberals and conservatives, echoed this concern. "Unless there is a change in United States policies in relation to the hemisphere," Figueres said, "there is the absurd possibility that Latin America may turn toward the Soviet Union."

Is the possibility indeed absurd? It would be even more absurd to ignore the realities behind it. From my own knowledge of the tremendous effort the Soviet Union has been making to outstrip the United States on all fronts and to penetrate underdeveloped nations everywhere, I have been convinced for years that Communism is a grave and growing problem for Latin America. It is a threat not to be minimized. The soil is present in which the seeds of Communism can grow at a frightening rate. There is Latin America's chronic anti-Americanism on which to build. Then there is its widespread poverty, its ignorance and illiteracy, its restlessness, its social backwardness and political instability. All have been and will continue to be exploited by the disciplined Communist parties and agents who know what they want and are determined to get it. A part of the problem is to persuade more Latin Americans to recognize that Communism is their problem as well as ours.

With the rise of Fidel Castro, Latin-American Communism has found itself a powerful ally in pressing on to its immediate goal. This is to frustrate all evolutionary solutions to Latin America's problems. It is to block all middle-of-the-road progress. It is to keep Latin America in turmoil. Above all, it is continuously and perpetually to disrupt good relations between the United States and the Latin-American republics.

"Fidelismo" has spread in varying degrees of meaning, intensity and power throughout this emotion-packed and problem-ridden region. It still has a tendency to break out here and there like a rash, rather than to show the monolithic character of the Communist movement. As a movement, it still has a long distance to go before it attains Castro's stated goal of "turning the Andes into the Sierra Maestra"—the stronghold from which he successfully waged his own rebellion in Cuba. But even in its present confused and complex character—a mixture of legitimate aspirations for land and other reforms plus extreme left-wing opportunism and extreme starry-eyed youthful idealism—it is developing an inner life that is so like the Communists' in method, aim and effects as to warrant the fear that they may fuse into a single force. The "Fidelistas" are willing to forego democracy—as a form of organization designed to slow down change; and they are willing to work with the Soviet Union and its Communist agents in Latin America.

Communist Organization in Latin America

Let me be more precise about the terms Communism and Communists. By Communists I do not mean reformers, or nationalists, or liberals, or radicals, or social democrats. Castro has appealed at one time or another, in varying degrees, to all of these. I do not even mean the non-Soviet varieties of Marxists. All of these groups are represented in large numbers in Latin America; and, unfortunately, at one time or another, many of them have been unwitting tools of the Communists. But I do not call them Communists. By Communist I mean someone who receives his orders via Moscow or Peking—someone who is dedicated to the ultimate world-wide victory of international Communism—and who works consciously, deliberately—patiently and everlastingly—toward that goal. This definitive standard of what is a Communist helps explain why the Communist leaders keep the party membership relatively small.

The Communist parties of Latin America were founded during the 1920's as replicas of the party in Soviet Russia, and with the direct assistance and participation of European Communists. As in the U.S.S.R. and throughout Europe, each party was subsequently purged of dissident elements and hammered into a tightly disciplined, ideologically rigid organization controlled and partially financed by Moscow. During the 1930's the Latin Communists followed Soviet leadership in opposing fascism and promoting "popular front" alliances with non-Communists of various persuasions. The first successful alliance of this type occurred in Chile in 1938 when Pedro Aguirre Cerda was elected President.

In 1939, when the Soviet Union signed a pact with Nazi Germany, the Latin-American Communists, along with all other Communists, reversed themselves immediately; they turned against their former friends of the non-Communist left and joined the Axis sympathizers and the native Latin-American fascists to harass the World War II activities of the western Allies. When Germany later invaded Russia, the Communists of Latin America completely reversed themselves again. The so-called "popular front" was forthwith enthusiastically revived.

It was during this second "popular front" phase that Latin-America Communists attained their greatest open and direct influence. They discouraged strikes and other activities which might slow the war effort; this won them the good will of industrialists and governmental leaders. They embraced in friendship and partnership all who opposed the Axis. They openly supported U.S.

and British objectives throughout Latin America. Thus the wartime alliance between the United States and the Soviet Union helped to break down the long-standing Latin-American prejudice against Communists. Thereafter, they were quick to capitalize on their new respectability.

This new, co-operative, patriotic spirit, set against the background of wartime emergency, accelerated the Communists' integration into national leadership. Their parties were declared legal in many countries and openly tolerated in most others. Batista, in Cuba, added Communists to his cabinet during the war. By 1945 and 1946, Communists held office as members of the national legislatures in Bolivia, Brazil, Chile, Colombia, Costa Rica, Cuba, Ecuador, Peru and Uruguay. In 1946 three Communists were elevated to the national cabinet in Chile. And even as late as 1960 the popular front movement survived in Chile to the point where 9 of the 45 members of the Chilean Senate and 21 of the 147 members of the Chamber of Deputies were members of the FRAP (Frente de Acción Popular), a coalition of three Marxist parties including the Communists. This Chilean "popular front," the only one of its kind surviving in Latin America during the past several years, fell short of winning first place by only about 35,000 votes in the last presidential election. A success in the next election by the Frapistas, as the coalition members are called, could establish an example for revival of the "popular front" formula elsewhere.

> [I continue to put the phrase "popular front" in quotation marks to remind the reader that it is a Communist propaganda phrase. It is typical of the Communist skill with words. They coin appealing phrases to sugar-coat or conceal their objectives. They have adopted and prostituted the great words of our language, such as freedom, democracy and justice—for which western men by the millions have bled and died. I was the first U.S. delegate at an international conference on freedom of information at Geneva in 1948 openly to denounce this notorious propaganda technique. Anne O'Hare McCormick later brilliantly characterized it as "upside-down language."]

The end of World War II, and the coming of the cold war, brought about a changed political climate in Latin America. The Communists then shifted over to their current strategy of parading as nationalists opposed to "Yanqui imperialism." Government after government tightened up in opposition to them. This came about not merely in anticipation of U.S. financial credits but because the primary loyalty of the Communists to the U.S.S.R. revealed itself once they had achieved responsible positions.

Their predominant strategy at present is a reversion to the technique of shifting alliances on the part of the openly arrived Communists, the party members, plus penetration by covert Communists and Communist sympathizers into non-Communist parties, into labor unions and student and women's organizations.

A recent report issued by Sen. Wayne Morse's subcommittee on American republics' affairs estimates the number of card-carrying Communist party members in Latin America at between 210,000 and 230,000 out of a total population of about 198,000,000. This number is substantially less than it was ten years ago and this fact has been interpreted in some quarters as a sign of Communist weakness.

But most qualified observers challenge such an interpretation. Camilo Ponce Enríquez, former President of Ecuador, told us: "The Communists are not threatening in terms of numbers but, like yeast, Communism germinates itself. The Communists are very adept at exploiting the masses who don't know where they are going or what they are up to. They know how to exploit dissatisfaction and how to direct it against the government."

The present Communist tactic seems to be to limit party membership to tightly organized activist groups, not a few of whose members have attended the Marx-Lenin school in Moscow where they have been thoroughly schooled in propaganda, subversion and espionage. (In tiny Costa Rica, for example, there are more than 200 Moscow-trained agitators.)

Some Other Communist Strategies and Techniques

One well-recognized technique of the Communist party, a tactic which does not require large numbers, is to instruct new recruits not to join the party but to become undercover members of left-wing democratic parties, where they are expected to organize "revolutionary" factions. The position taken by these factions normally coincides with the Communist party line. At present, for example, this line is to support Castro against U.S. "imperialism." This tactic has been used with varying degrees of success in Venezuela (Democratic Action party), Colombia and Honduras (Liberal party), Argentina and Uruguay (Socialist party), Peru (Alianza Popular Revolucionaria Americana [APRA] and Costa Rica (National Liberation party).

The Latin-American Communists often have gained influence through the skill of their maneuvering. During his campaign, President Frondizi of Argentina did not disavow full Communist support. Although he publicly denounced the Communists after his election, the opposition People's Radical party claims that the Communists are still around and that they have access to the president. In Brazil Vice-Pres. João Goulart is closely identified with the Communists. They supported him in 1960 in his victorious campaign for re-election. (They also officially supported Marshal Henrique Teixeira Lott, the administration candidate for president, though he had occasionally criticized their stand publicly and had reaffirmed Brazil's place with the West. Marshal Lott was defeated.)

When the Communists have considered it expedient they have not hesitated to make alliances with right-wing dictators. Such combinations are not so strange as they might seem at first glance; Communists and dictators have a mutual interest in stifling and eradicating democratic influences. In exchange for supporting a dictator, Communists may receive official tolerance. They may even be given a free hand to infiltrate the labor movement. At one time or another, various Latin-American dictators have welcomed Communist assistance, among them Perón of

Argentina, Manuel Odría of Peru and Pérez Jiménez of Venezuela. Even Generalissimo Trujillo of the Dominican Republic, who made much of his opposition to Communists, was glad to have their help on occasion.

One form of the Communists' strategy, when a dictatorship is in power, is to split themselves into two distinct groups, seemingly independent of one another. One group allies itself with the dictator, grasping every advantage to be gained by open and direct association with the government in power. The second group goes underground and maintains an uncompromising opposition to the dictator. It works to infiltrate and dominate the non-Communist opposition forces. When a revolution takes place and the dictator is overthrown, the first group merely fades away, while the second does its utmost to guide and control the revolution.

In fact, it was a reactionary dictatorship which paved the way for Latin America's first Communist regime. For years, Guatemala was ruled by the right-wing dictator Gen. Jorge Ubico. His government opposed such measures as social security, the improvement of working conditions and agrarian reform. He labeled these "Communistic," and smeared the reformers as "Communists." The dictator himself thus gave the Communists a reputation for sound reform which they never could have attained on their own.

Nonetheless, the Communists were a minority among those who opposed Ubico. When revolution came in 1944 it was not a Communist revolution but one patterned after the objectives of the Mexican revolution of three decades before. Not until Jacobo Arbenz was elected president in 1951 did the Communists come into power; and, even then, they were but one party in a coalition of parties which comprised the new government. However, every other party in the coalition had been infiltrated with Communists and partially staffed by undercover members of the Communist party. The Guatemalan Communists then betrayed the goals of the 1944 revolution and took over. Then the issue of Communist activity in the government served as the spark for still another revolution, which in turn overthrew the Arbenz regime in 1954. I believe most thoughtful Guatemalans now understand how Communists are willing to distort for their own ends—the ends of disrupting inter-American relations—the social goals of a democratic revolution.

The current President of Guatemala, Miguel Ydígoras Fuentes, explained to us that of the 2,000 who fled the country in 1954 after Arbenz was overthrown—many of whom were Communists—he has permitted about 1,000 to return, a few at a time. A good many of these returned exiles have abandoned communism and are now participating constructively in Guatemala's national life. All of them are permitted their freedom when they return. President Ydígoras spoke of a former foreign minister who, upon his return, drew an audience of 1,500 at his first lecture, about 500 at his second, and only 50 at his third. After a few more attempts, this man voluntarily left the country.

Many throughout Latin America seem still to suspect that the United States "engineered" the overthrow of Arbenz "in defense of the United Fruit Co." and that the charge of communism was a red herring invented by the U.S. State Department. This allegation is often cited as an instance of U.S. support of opposition to reform. The allegation is an evidence of failure in our communication with Latin America, for the case is clear cut. The conduct of the Communists in Guatemala is one more instance of the cold and callous nature of their purpose: they are primarily seeking not reform but the disruption of inter-American concord in line with policies laid down in Moscow.

The Communists of Latin America have of course sometimes been neglected by Moscow, and many are still Stalinists, indifferent to the latest currents across the "iron curtain." Further, with a few exceptions in Mexico, Chile and Brazil, they have not recruited the corps of intellectuals that have given distinction to the Communist parties of France and Italy. And I do not mean to suggest that they have not made many political mistakes. Their callousness in playing both sides of the fence in the countries of dictatorship has not passed unnoticed; neither has their abandonment of "progressive" programs in the hope that this might embarrass the United States.

More on Anti-Americanism

U.S. baiting is an old story in Latin America. It began long before either Castro or communism appeared on the scene. Both are now capitalizing skillfully on the anti-U.S. sentiment they inherited.

Credit: Cornell Capa—Magnum Photos

Soldiers and guns were required to maintain order on the streets of Lima, Peru, during the elections of 1956.

For generations, too few in the U.S. have tried to understand the Latin mind and temperament or its cultural achievements. Because we have been relatively unconcerned about Latin-American affairs, our southern neighbors have felt that they were often put on a lower rung of the diplomatic ladder. Tannenbaum has pointed out that the problem is made deep and difficult because the people of the United States, unhappily, do in fact feel superior to the people of Latin America—and the Latin Americans know it.

Historically, the Latin people have feared and envied the United States. They would like to share our high standard of living. But their leaders have been traditionally suspicious of the methods by which we have achieved this standard, and, as Tannenbaum suggests, they have not been strongly motivated to change their way of life in order to push the industrialization program required for a higher standard for all. They have hoped to achieve the new industrialization without changing the old way of life. Further, they have resented what they deem foreign influence in their political and economic affairs, and most notably U.S. influence.

The Communists capitalize on this background by persistently and skillfully playing up the anti-imperialist, anti-Yanqui theme. Alberto Lleras Camargo, President of Colombia, told us: "The Communists operate in South America primarily to embarrass and upset the United States—and to discredit the United States throughout the world by showing that the United States cannot even get along with its closest neighbors."

Party members regard propaganda as a major function. Informed sources told me that in the state of São Paulo there are 5,400 card-carrying Communists operating in about 300 cells. Their immediate goal is to isolate Brazil from the U.S. and develop closer ties between Brazil and the Soviet Union. A leading Brazilian industrialist told me that 35,000 persons were taking a 48-lesson course of study, six nights a week, in the principles of Marxism and Leninism under the tutelage of the Communist party. Lesson No. 23 is said to be especially interesting to a visitor from the United States. It is reportedly entitled: "How to Throw the Americans out of Brazil!"

Thus the Communists clamor loudly for "nationalism" in Latin America; they oppose foreign investment as an instrument of imperialism and label efforts by the United States and international financial agencies to stabilize money and inhibit inflation as "intervention." It is of course ironic that the Communists can continually and actively intervene in Latin-American affairs, all the while masquerading as "nationalists." But this is a pattern the Communists have followed elsewhere with success. The Soviet Union seems far away to many Latin Americans—and the "colossus of the north" troubled them long before the birth of Nikita Khrushchev.

One common misconception fomented by the Communists in Latin America is that United States and other foreign private industry is skimming the cream off Latin America's great wealth in natural resources, and funneling huge profits abroad. Governor Stevenson and I were told by a group opposing the current administration in Chile, for example, that the major U.S. mining companies were given treatment more favorable than that given the Chilean companies, and that the main result was to siphon abroad much of Chile's natural wealth. Statistics were quoted. But we were unable to confirm the existence of any special treatment. Top-ranking Chilean officials told us that approximately 60% of the gross earnings of the U.S. mining companies in Chile goes to the Chilean government in taxes, adding more than $100,000,000 annually to the Chilean budget. This is, of course, over and above salaries and wages, transportation costs and other payments that go back into the Chilean economy.

The image of U.S. industrialists as "bloodsucking leeches" is thus carefully fostered by the Communists. In a 1958 interview with a Brazilian journalist, Khrushchev spelled out this Communist line clearly: "For decades the American, British and other foreign monopolies, like giant leeches, have been clinging to the living body of Latin America, greedily sucking dry and plundering its natural wealth, ruthlessly exploiting its peoples, distorting their economies and retarding their natural development."

This is strong stuff. But it strikes a sympathetic chord in Latin America where, as I pointed out in the previous section, a stubborn misunderstanding persists about the function of private

—as opposed to government—capital. Starting from Latin America's historic hostility to "capitalist exploitation," red propagandists move easily to the standard Marxist formula about "economic imperialism," including the slogan about the "warmongering" of the capitalists as they seek to protect their markets and their investments.

Something About How Red Propaganda Operates

An extensive network of propaganda and cultural operations has been created to exploit and to deepen this anti-U.S. feeling, and to extol the achievements of the Communist bloc countries.

The Soviet Union is pouring large sums of money into this network. Estimates of these sums run as high as $100,000,000 a year. And this is in addition to the propaganda funds raised by the Latin-American Communists themselves through local contributions and levies on their memberships. This figure of $100,000,000 approximates the total budget of the United States Information agency for the entire globe. Thus the Soviets are spending many times as much for propaganda in Latin America as is the United States. Further, the $100,000,000 estimate does not include the cost of short-wave broadcasting to Latin America from the U.S.S.R., China and the east European satellites. At the close of 1959 the Soviet bloc was beaming 138 hours a week to Latin America (compared with 33 hours in 1955). Two hours a week are directed in the Quechua language to the 5,000,000 Indians in Ecuador, Peru and Bolivia who speak that tongue; these broadcasts concentrate not so much on the achievements of the Soviets or China as on land reform and other Indian problems.

In addition to the short-wave programs from abroad, Communist radio programs are carried on local stations in at least ten Latin-American countries, with time purchased either by Communist bloc diplomatic missions or by local Communist parties. They also buy television time in some countries. News, music, entertainment and cultural programs are featured on such programs. Occasionally Soviet bloc commercial products are advertised. Many of the programs are "packaged shows" produced in bloc countries.

Distribution of Communist bloc films also has increased. During 1958, among the 20 Latin-American countries all but 7—these exceptions were all Central American and Caribbean countries—are known to have exhibited Soviet bloc films. In the same year, bloc film festivals were held in Argentina, Chile, Colombia, Ecuador, Uruguay and Venezuela. None had been reported for the previous year.

The printing press continues to be a potent weapon in the hands of the red propagandists. Communist literature and Communist periodicals abound in Latin America. Some newsstands in the major cities are loaded with Communist literature. Three daily newspapers—*Hoy* ("Today") in Havana, now printed on Cuban government presses, *El Siglo* ("The Century") in Santiago, Chile, and a Portuguese-language daily in São Paulo—plus the Communist weekly newspapers, comprise the hard core of the Communist press.

There is a network of red book-publishing organizations. The 1958 catalogue of the Communist book-publishing house in Montevideo, Ediciones Pueblos Unidos, S.A., listed about 1,200 titles by Communist writers, including Chinese and east European as well as Soviet writers.

Senator Morse's committee estimates that over 300 Communist and pro-Communist periodicals are currently available in Latin America, about 100 of them printed abroad and the balance produced locally. Some periodicals are distributed through trade unions and student organizations. The editors warn their governments against co-operating with the U.S. in military matters. As "proof" of U.S. aggressive intentions they hammer at vast U.S. military expenditures, at our "constant refusal" to accept Soviet disarmament proposals and at our guided missile program. The Communist press even blamed U.S. atomic testing for the 1960 floods in Uruguay and the earthquakes in Chile.

One function of the Communist propagandists in Mexico is to operate the Institute of Cultural Exchange between the U.S.S.R.

and Mexico. In one typical month, this institute had three evening meetings with large attendance; it conducted regular classes in the Russian language; it distributed a Soviet propaganda book published in Spanish; and it prompted the distribution of low-cost editions of Russian classics by Pushkin, Chekhov and Tolstoi.

This Mexican center is part of a Latin network. In 1958 there were 84 active Communist-bloc "cultural centers," so-called friendship societies (and *émigré* centers notably for "overseas Chinese"), in operation in Latin America. This was 40 more than had been in existence in 1957. These centers cover a wide range of interests. Some emphasize music, some others literature, others art, or all of these fields together. Some are active in arranging for the exchange of cultural groups and exhibits, and for the dissemination of bloc literature.

There were 36 Communist-bloc cultural and industrial exhibits in Latin America in 1958. In the same year, 13 Latin-American exhibits were welcomed to bloc countries, most of them also involving invitations to Latin-American artists to visit the exhibits.

On occasion, the Soviets participate openly and directly in a major cultural offensive. An example is the recent Soviet exhibition in Mexico City, visited by Deputy Premier A. I. Mikoyan, which cost the Soviets at least $450,000—plus salaries for the Mexicans engaged in the project, plus the full-time work of most of the staff in the Soviet embassy, and other expenses.

There are 125 Soviet citizens in the U.S.S.R. embassy in Mexico City, as compared with 4 Mexicans in the Mexican embassy in Moscow. On a day said to be chosen at random—January 20, 1960—a check was made on the amount of mail sent from this Soviet embassy. In just that one day, 750,000 pieces of mail, weighing a total of 20,000 lb., went out to Cuba alone. This may give some idea of the extent of Soviet printed material developed for Latin America.

I am particularly alarmed by the Communist progress with promising young people. Again and again I heard that students were being given free trips to the U.S.S.R. and even to China. The declared objective was to provide an educational and cultural experience; the real objective, of course, was to impress these young people with the Soviet way of life, as opposed to

Credit: Mazo Brothers

Soviet Deputy Premier Anastas Mikoyan cutting the tape to open the U.S.S.R. exhibition in Mexico City in 1960. At left is President López Mateos of Mexico.

the western way. In the one year of 1959 the Russians are reported to have spent $900,000 just for airplane tickets to transport Latin-American students to the U.S.S.R. Several times I was introduced to students and professors who had recently returned from China. Juan Gómez Millas, the Rector of the University of Chile, was leaving for China the week we were in Santiago.

(These visits to China were symptoms of a new Chinese propaganda drive in Latin America which we were told has been developing rapidly. Discussion of this drive suggested that it may reflect the growing rivalry for control of Communism between China and the U.S.S.R. More likely is the theory that both powers have agreed that the pattern of China's Communization may prove applicable to Latin America as much or even more than the pattern followed in the U.S.S.R.)

Here are two paragraphs of Senator Morse's committee report on the progress of Soviet propaganda in Latin America:

> There is no doubt that the Soviet Union and its satellites are making a major (and intensifying) effort to impress the Latin American countries with their cultural, scientific and production accomplishments, and to promote friendship. . . .
>
> The Soviet offensive in the political and cultural spheres has had a significant impact, even though 17 of these 20 countries still withhold diplomatic recognition of the Soviet Union. Soviet prestige has risen in Latin America just as it has in the United States, Western Europe, and elsewhere. Soviet supremacy in rocketry, and its notable accomplishments in other areas of science and technology, and in economic development, obviously impress peoples who in these respects are far behind. Its international political position and power are facts to be faced.

More on Communist Infiltration in the Latin Labor Movement

In every case, whether they are operating in the open or underground, a prime objective of the Communists is to take over the labor movement. More than 1,000,000 labor union members in Latin America are said to be under the domination of Communist leadership. The tactics employed are familiar. For a period they were used with conspicuous success in the United States. Rarely do the Communists place one of their party members in a top spot. Instead, such places are filled by a friendly "democratic" labor leader. The key positions near the top—the executive committee posts—are then captured by hard-core Communists. Once entrenched, they work hard on trade-union matters which will gain them the support of the non-Communist rank and file.

In many countries the workers have become disillusioned, then desperate, as they have watched inflation wipe out the value of their wage increases and their savings. This has bred a growing cynicism toward the whole democratic system. The Communists trumpet to workers, "Our system is the only one that works—the only one that can accomplish real economic progress for the working man."

Early in 1959 the United Confederation of Labour of Chile (CUTCH), which is under Communist control, launched an appeal for the organization of a so-called "third force" (another clever Communist phrase), restricted to Latin-American unions and excluding those from Canada, the United States and the British and Netherlands West Indies. A preliminary meeting was supposed to be held in Caracas, Venezuela, with the co-operation of the provisional committee of the reorganized Venezuelan labor movement, which included Communist elements and many fellow travelers. However, the idea did not then prosper because of—among other factors—opposition from democratic trade unionists in Venezuela itself. Even the Cuban Confederation of Labor (CTC) opposed at that time the idea of such a "third force."

However, at the CTC convention held in November 1959 the Communists managed to obtain the disaffiliation of the CTC from the non-Communist International Confederation of Free Trade Unions and its regional western hemisphere branch, ORIT. At the same time they launched a plan for organizing a Latin-American confederation of labor under "democratic revolutionary leadership," to supplant and absorb the existing regional labor groups. With Raúl Castro, Fidel's brother, taking the lead, all key figures in the Castro regime are now backing this Communist-led "third force" movement. If it succeeds it will be one of the most significant services the Castro regime can render to communism. The Cubans attempted to start their "third force" with the organization of a Central American federation of labor. A meeting was held in San Salvador at the end of April 1960. But no union affiliated to ORIT allowed itself to be inveigled into participating. Only known Communist delegates attended and the conference itself was deemed a failure.

In Brazil, at the National Labor convention held in August 1960, the Communists almost gained control and were about to win support for a "third force" proposal when the democratic leaders walked out, followed by most of the delegates.

The arguments that the Communists and their fellow travelers advance in support of this "third force" are based on three concepts: nationalism, neutralism and unity. All have considerable support among the Latin-American masses.

Nationalism is used as an argument to convince the Latin-American unionists that they need to stick together without mixing with North Americans with whom, the Communists say, they have nothing in common. The purpose of this appeal is to insulate the Latin-American unions from North American influence and thus make them easier prey for Communist infiltration and domination.

Neutralism is an argument skillfully manipulated by the Communists who point out that the Latin-American unions should steer clear of the east-west conflict because they have nothing to gain from taking sides.

Unity is advanced by the Communists as an argument to counteract the well-known policy of democratic trade unions of opposing collaboration with the Communists. When this point is debated before a politically immature audience, not schooled in the Communist use of catch phrases, the Communists often manage to score. The slogan of "unity regardless of race, color, religion, political views, etc." sounds better, and has often proved easier to put across, than the appeal which calls for "unity regardless of race, color, religion but not with the Communists or any other brand of totalitarianism."

The AFL-CIO hailed the overthrow of the Batista dictatorship in Cuba and pledged its friendship and assistance to the incoming government. But U.S. labor has greatly altered its opinion of Castro and his regime—so much so that, on May 4, 1960, the AFL-CIO executive council issued a perceptive statement which featured these conclusions:

> . . . The latest manifestations of the Castro regime have revealed unmistakable signs of a definite trend toward a totalitarian state. This is based upon the technique of regimentation and militarization of the masses to a degree comparable to the practices prevailing under fascist or communist regimes.
>
> The Cuban Confederation of Labor has become a mere appendage of the Government under complete control of pro-communist elements imposed from above without consideration of the will of the rank and file.
>
> Loyalty to democratic principles and opposition to communism has been branded by the Castro government as synonymous with counter-revolutionary activity, punishable with discharge from the job, immediate arrest, and loss of property.
>
> The right of collective bargaining has been abolished. As in countries behind the Iron Curtain, Cuban workers are no longer free to change jobs without government approval. Hiring and firing have become the prerogative of the government. The quest for economic improvement, a legitimate trade union activity, has been banned.

This official AFL-CIO statement then assesses Castro and his regime as follows:

> The disruptive activities of the Cuban Government can no longer be lightly dismissed as the outburst of inexperienced youthful leaders swept by the upsurge of economic nationalism. They have all the earmarks of a well planned strategy designed to make Cuba an advanced outpost of the Soviet Union's drive to infiltrate the New World.

To summarize, we can be sure that the drive for the "third force" will not be abandoned. Further, I feel that the Communist threat on the Latin-American labor front is so serious that, if such policy suited the Soviet Union, Communist-induced strikes and sabotage could interfere seriously with the flow of goods from Latin America to the United States. This would prove critically damaging in time of war.

Cuba—Red Beachhead in the Western Hemisphere

Adolf Berle, former U.S. Ambassador to Brazil and one of the wisest and most experienced U.S. students of Latin-America, wrote during the summer of 1960:

> For all practical purposes, Cuba is just as much a Communist satellite as Hungary or North Korea. I mean that a few communists, or men controlled by them, whose policy and tactics are directed either by Moscow or Peking . . . are in control of Cuba's resources, its territory, and its voiceless people.

Nothing in the record of Soviet activities I have been outlining equals for aggressiveness Premier Khrushchev's startling (and wholly gratuitous) threat in midsummer 1960 to retaliate with red rockets if the United States were to intervene militarily in Cuba. Though he later modified it by calling it "symbolic," that was a shout that made the $100,000,000 propaganda operation seem like a whisper campaign by comparison. I believe it finally convinced many in the other 19 Latin republics of what President Eisenhower called "the clear intention [of the U.S.S.R.] to establish Cuba in a role serving Soviet purposes in this hemisphere."

It was Castro's acceptance of the Khrushchev offer of military as well as economic help that set the alarm bells ringing even in those government offices of Latin America most friendly to Castro. The Cuban expropriation of U.S. property had not been unexpected, and Castro's tirades against the U.S. were not very far outside the Latin revolutionary pattern. But the open alliance with Moscow was new and ominous.

Three theories had been discussed by Latin-American leaders we talked with during the early months of 1960. One pictured Castro as a particularly emotional dictator-reformer who was definitely non-Communist and who was using such Communist aides as Ernesto "Che" Guevara for his own purposes. A second theory had him attempting the Nasser role of playing one great power against another. The third pictured him as a full-fledged instrument of the Kremlin. The swift events of the summer focused the discussion on points two and three. As this book goes to press, it is increasingly clear that the AFL-CIO was right in its May 4 statement—that Cuba is now indeed "an advance outpost of the Soviet Union's drive to infiltrate the New World." However, as events developed in 1960 predictions that Castro's government would founder on the rocks of economic shortage were being tempered. If he can supply the eggs and the chickens, the rice and the chemicals, and can develop new trade relationships which can furnish Cuba with export markets and import needs, he could survive in Cuba for many years to come—if he can escape assassination!

To understand the background, it is important to recall that the Communists had little to do with the revolution in Cuba until well after the overthrow of Batista. Berle points out that "for a substantial period of time the aggregate morale of the Cuban revolution was democratic, anti-dictatorial and anti-communist." In line with their established techniques, the Communists moved in and took over after the revolution had come to power.

Cuba has long been a center of activity for Latin-American communism. On November 7, 1933, the anniversary of the Bolshevik revolution in Russia, the Cuban Communists attempted a revolution of their own. Their most important victory, perhaps, was the establishment of a full-fledged "Soviet" in Oriente province. Peasants seized the land they had been working, and a Communist regime backed by a militia of "red guards" took control. This Communist experiment lasted for several months.

It was the dictator overthrown by Castro—Fulgencio Batista—who legalized the Communist party in Cuba. Indeed, in line with their frequent tactic of co-operation with dictators, the Communists did not shift their support from Batista to Castro until 1958, five years after the Castro movement began. Batista first permitted the Communists to found a newspaper, *Hoy*, which began publication on May Day, 1938, and is still being published. Later that same year, Batista called in newspapermen for a press conference and announced: "The Communist party, accord-

ing to its constitution, is a democratic party which pursues its ends within the framework of a capitalist regime and renounces violence as a political means, and consequently it is entitled to the same status as that of any other party in Cuba." On September 25, 1938, the Communist party, operating under that name, became legal in Cuba for the first time.

Subsequent years saw more gains for communism in Cuba. In the elections of July 1940, ten Communists were elected to the National Chamber of Deputies, and a Communist was elected mayor of the second largest city in the republic, Santiago de Cuba. In March 1943 Juan Marinello, a prominent intellectual and Communist leader, was named minister without portfolio in the national government—the first Communist to attain cabinet rank in any of the Latin-American republics. Moreover, Batista permitted the Communists to infiltrate the labor movement and even to exert power in the ministry of labor.

Thus a cohesive and skilled Communist nucleus existed which was capable of seizing the moment when it came. The Communists were not alone in waiting for it. Hundreds of thousands of Cubans, including a substantial percentage of intellectuals, felt that Castro's case against the political and social system of Cuba was justified in democratic terms and a substantial proportion still believe his case against the U.S. is a good one. The Communists did not create the Castro revolution, but they were very quick to exploit it.

"*Fidelistas*"

It is becoming increasingly clear that Fidel Castro is determined that there shall be more Cubas in Latin America. A leading instrument at his disposal—and at the disposal of the Soviet Union—is the Cuban diplomatic corps.

The Soviet Union has only four embassies in Latin America. Cuba has diplomatic representatives throughout, and Cuban representatives, being at home in the Latin-American cultural milieu, can hope for a greater intimacy with the local scene than any Russian is likely to achieve. When Castro came to power, he discharged the experienced career diplomats in Cuban embassies and replaced them with ardent young leftists, some of whom are only 26 or 27 years old; the new Cuban Ambassador to Argentina is 30. Many if not all of these new diplomatic representatives are Communist oriented. They can utilize their diplomatic privileges and prerogatives to aid international communism. For instance, they can collect intelligence reports for the U.S.S.R. They can transmit funds and instructions from the Soviets to local Communist leaders via the diplomatic pouches which enjoy immunity. One of our ambassadors said to me flatly that the local Cuban ambassador was so obvious in his pro-Soviet activities that whenever he returned from a visit to Havana he checked in at the Soviet embassy before going to his own office in the Cuban embassy. (Of course, if such Communist subversive activities become too pronounced, there is the probability that many Latin countries will clamp down and shut up the embassies.)

A new press service, Prensa Latina, has been established by the Castro regime to distribute "news stories" throughout Latin America. This agency echoes the line of the Communist newspapers. In addition, Castro is now building a powerful radio transmitter to drench Latin America with his oral propaganda, and is supplementing it with his exported printed propaganda material featuring the message: "Our revolution is your revolution! What are you doing, Comrade, in your own country?" No opportunity to drive home this message is overlooked. When Castro sent relief supplies to victims of the earthquakes in Chile, Chilean officials found that with the bags of sugar and piles of clothing were intermixed propaganda leaflets. Among them was Ernesto Guevara's *The War of Guerrillas* which offers a blueprint for revolution "in our America" and which has become something of a best seller in certain Latin-American circles.

Throughout Latin America, "Defense of Cuba" and "Friends of Cuba" committees have been formed which could easily be turned into insurrectionist groups. From northern Peru come reports of "Fidelista" rifle clubs. These groups include Communists as well as other members who have broken away from the country's strongest party, the left wing but anti-Communist APRA.

In the autumn of 1960 the governments of Guatemala and Nicaragua were shaken by rebel movements which they said were directly inspired by Castro and his "Fidelistas" and probably armed from his arsenal of Soviet and Czechoslovak weapons. In nearby Salvador, where a ruling elite of coffee growers and the military was thrown out in the fall of 1960 by a bloodless coup, there were strong indications that young men in the new governing junta have warm sympathies for Castro and his methods.

> [In the fall of 1960, President Eisenhower sent a U.S. fleet to cruise off the coasts of the threatened countries for several weeks and to embargo any illicit flow of arms.
>
> Further, Venezuela came to the front as a major area vulnerable to the "Fidelistas." Here, an alliance of students and workers staged their second major riot in a month against the freely elected regime of Pres. Rómulo Betancourt. They demanded alliance with Cuba, the ouster of foreign oil companies and radical land reform on the Cuban pattern, instead of the careful system of land distribution and organized rural credit that was being attempted by the government.]

Another area sensitive to the "Fidelistas" is British Guiana, which borders on Venezuela and looks out toward Cuba across the Caribbean. Guiana has no "Fidelista" movement by that precise name, but it has a social and political equivalent in a movement centered around the person of Chief Minister Cheddi B. Jagan. Far left in his politics, Jagan owed his 1953 election to the crushing poverty of the colony's sugar workers. Embittered recently by the failure of his negotiations with the British for autonomy and by what he regarded as insufficient British aid to Guiana, Jagan went to Havana and promptly obtained a $5,000,000 loan from Castro.

A further major country vulnerable to the "Fidelistas" is Bolivia, with its own blight of misery in the heart of the South American continent. Despite the social revolution which came eight years ago, and despite government control of the all-important tin mines and the existence of armed workers' militias, the social and economic shake-up has not been nearly so complete as in Cuba. Financial and technical aid from the United States has kept Bolivia from collapse throughout this period, and has helped support the structure of the country's democratic institutions. Yet the "Fidelistas" within the National Revolutionary movement of Pres. Víctor Paz Estenssoro are busily turning the strong current of anti-American sentiment to their own antidemocratic use. Reportedly, they are getting help, including funds, from the Cuban ambassador.

Another major area vulnerable to the "Fidelistas" is the northeastern corner of Brazil. This region of nearly 500,000 sq.mi. and 20,000,000 inhabitants is parched by droughts and has been condemned for centuries to virtual subhuman misery. Here, the fast-growing Peasant league is the carrier of "Fidelismo," with its own "little Fidel" in the person of Francisco Julião. A lawyer, small landowner and novelist, Julião attracted a following at first by his humanitarian campaign to protect peasants and argue their cases in contests with the owners of the great landed estates. The Peasant league he formed for this purpose originally had no political overtones. But in the spring of 1960, Julião went to Havana, saw Castro's experiment and came back with new ideas. He initiated a rapid expansion in the number of league offices, collected a number of affiliate organizations, won over university student bodies, formed cadres of professional indoctrinators and troupes of political minstrels. The sum of it all is a revolutionary political movement of great fervor, loudly devoted to land reform —and to proclaiming the virtues of Castro and Mao Tse-tung.

All of the areas where "Fidelismo" is a clear and present danger have in common a record of years of neglect and poverty that recent efforts at reform have had no chance or time to overcome. Yet the quick and widespread acceptance of naked communism will be held back by a number of factors—the spirited individualism that is a dominant quality of Latin America, the influence of the church and the sheer distance from the great capitals of communism. The Communist pattern used in the take-over of Czechoslovakia, which had Red armies on its borders, seems only a remote possibility. Yet the Communists can take vast strides towards their objectives in many areas of Latin America by the promotion of the Trojan horse of "Fidelismo."

Many Latin-American political leaders hailed Castro in the early stages of his ascent to power. The students and people were originally enthusiastic. Castro's later conduct, notably his executions and censorship, cooled off most leaders, while men of cabinet rank in half a dozen countries now shrug him off as a mental case featuring an "infantile quality." But his appeal and the appeal of his revolutionary ideas are still widespread and must be reckoned with in any appraisal of the Communist danger. Indeed, this appeal will cause some political candidates in other countries to continue to woo him. Thus when the conference of foreign ministers met in Costa Rica in August 1960, many of the political leaders present were reluctant to single out Cuba by name, even though they were willing to condemn Communist interference in the western hemisphere and to condemn the willingness of any hemisphere nation to accept Communist military aid. (This latter element in the declaration of San José technically put Castro in a position of isolation.) While we were in Brazil, Jânio Quadros, then the leading aspirant to the presidency and later elected to succeed Kubitschek, took a notable party of his supporters to visit Castro. When I asked one of the senators in the party why Quadros was going, he replied, "Every time Quadros mentions Castro's name in a speech, the people cheer!" Castro is not only identified in the minds of the voters with land reform, but he tossed out one of the hated dictators. Further, he wins popularity by thumbing his nose at the United States.

Without exception the political leaders of Latin America with whom we discussed Castro and Cuba approved of the early moderation and restraint exercised by the U.S. government–under most extraordinary provocation. Without exception, they would oppose any overt United States military intervention.

However, there is a growing sentiment among Latin-American political leaders for collective intervention in such instances as the one which led to the breaking of diplomatic relations with, and the application of sanctions against, the Trujillo regime in the Dominican Republic. President Betancourt, in a telegram to OAS general secretary, José A. Mora, made a proposal for submission to the next inter-American conference, being held in Quito, Ecuador, in 1961. Betancourt proposed that the conference formulate a treaty which would clearly bar any government from the regional groups which is "not elected by the people." This was interpreted as a warning for Cuba, which has not had elections since Castro came to power.

Betancourt also proposed that the OAS require member governments to recognize individual human rights and guarantee freedom of the press and the right of political opposition. He believes that a basic step will be taken toward eradicating dictatorship from this hemisphere when the "promoters of coups" realize that a violent seizure of power and subsequent dictatorship will be met with "an asphyxiating ring of isolation" and by withdrawal of recognition.

The extent to which the Communists will succeed in their aims under the cover of "Fidelismo"—or in open alliance with it—will depend on several things. It will depend in very considerable degree on the extent to which Latin-American governments and the elite sectors of their societies fail to launch effective programs to ease the misery so widely prevailing and fail to satisfy the growing nationalism. Castro himself is convinced that this failure is bound to occur, and that Cuba will be the revolutionary hub of the movement that will take over after the failure. He might not need more than a few victories in countries going "the Cuban way" to produce a chain reaction of victories throughout much of the Latin-American world.

As things now stand, the tenpins may be set up in his bowling alley more clearly than we are willing to admit. Most Latin-American governments, which are largely made up of political moderates, see the future of their countries in terms of evolutionary economic development. Yet all of them face a tangle of problems which are complicated by sustained Communist-inspired attacks on every effort at economic stabilization in their inflation-ridden economies. It seems unlikely that they will be able to get very far in their evolutionary approach without very substantial outside help—meaning, specifically, help from the United States.

Timing will be of the utmost importance. Let us assume that reasonable economic and social development and the raising of living standards may be the antidotes to "Fidelismo"—and hence to communism. Even so, in the face of left-wing agitation and the disruptive bite of inflation, will there be time to put the necessary programs into effect, even with massive United States assistance? This may turn out to be the key question.

If the answer is in the negative, then we had better brace ourselves against the worst. One of the ablest U.S. students of Latin America wrote me late in 1960: "The situation could explode and go over the dam in several places. Just now there is a moment of shuddering indecision waiting to see whether the United States will pick up a line and start going. If it does not, there will be explosion after explosion all over Hispanic America." Such a triumph of "Fidelismo" will lead to the emergence of bitterly anti-U.S. governments which will proceed to walk the path charted by Castro: first the assaults on U.S. property, then confiscation in the name of patriotism, then appeals to Communist nations for economic aid "to develop the country without strings attached," then neutralism, followed by a foreign policy alignment with Moscow and Peking.

This sequence is by no means inevitable. But if the chain is to be broken the people of the United States must become clear in their own minds that the contest for Latin America is now drawn in terms of "revolution" and "evolution"—and that these terms in turn are now embodied on the one side by Cuban "Fidelismo," in firm alliance with communism, and on the other side by the moderates of Latin America who hope for understanding and aid from the United States.

In Latin America, as in Asia and Africa, the Communists have not created the conditions of poverty and restlessness in which they flourish—any more than they created Castro. They exploit conditions that already exist or they promote developments which suit their purposes. Through their network of well-disciplined agents they are always ready and able to take advantage of local situations, such as has developed in Cuba. The party line may appear to zigzag sharply, sometimes supporting a program in one country that it is fighting in another. Nonetheless, the constant aim of the Communists is to neutralize the entire continent of Latin America and remove it from the western orbit. This makes the Communists the United States' principal problem and enemy in Latin America—as they are throughout the world.

4

Education—The Key to Latin America's Future

Five years ago, I reported on a trip to the Soviet Union and East Europe I had taken the previous autumn. Part of my report was devoted to the undoubted achievements of the Communist regime in training its young people. In less than 40 years, beginning with a population of whom half to three-quarters were illiterate, the U.S.S.R. had built an educational training system rivaling that of the United States in universality.

"If the Soviets gave up butter for guns," I wrote, "they gave up meat for education."

I was struck especially by the determination of the Soviet hierarchy that no shred of talent which might serve the state should go undeveloped; by the rigor of the curriculum and the intensity of the students' dedication to it, at all levels from primary school through the university; and by the rewards opened up for careers in science, scholarship and advanced technology, including financial incentives and rewards which rival those which we of the west offer our corporation presidents.

Many of my readers seemed startled by my description of the curriculum of the basic ten-year school which the Soviet authorities then intended to open up to every Soviet boy and girl. The curriculum required ten years of mathematics, six years of a foreign language, five years of physics, four of chemistry and four of biology, along with history, literature and other academic subjects. Competition for entrance into the universities was so keen that millions attended night schools for years in order to make the grade. And far from paying tuition, the university students received generous stipends, plus draft exemption, plus a guarantee of top jobs on graduation.

Thus when the first sputnik soared into orbit in 1957, followed by Major Gagarin in 1961, those who had studied Soviet education understood that it was a challenge to the United States not merely in the field of rocketry but across the board in education and research.

The Great Gap and the Great Hope

Nothing could be more startling—and dismaying—than the contrast I found between the Soviet educational and training system and that which prevails—or does not prevail—in the Latin-American republics. I have discussed the Communist threat in Latin America. Part of that threat is the glittering Soviet example of its educational progress. This example is now ready to the hands of Communist propagandists in Latin America. The question it poses is whether Latin America, by democratic means, can sufficiently widen and deepen its educational opportunities.[1]

In my judgment, the present yawning gap between the universality—and the intensity—of the Soviet system and the Latin system must be narrowed—and dramatically—and soon. Expenditures for education in Latin America now range from a low of $2.00 per person a year in Haiti, Peru and Paraguay to a high

[1] There can of course be no doubt that the stated aim of Latin-American education—the development of each individual—will continue to be superior to the Communist aim of service to the state. Further, I do not deny that some Latin-American centers of learning are now distinguished. For example, taking Brazil only, the University of Bahia offers outstanding opportunities in music as does the University of São Paulo in medicine and Mackenzie College in architecture.

of $11.00 in Argentina and Chile. These compare with a national average of about $70.00 in the U.S. (figures for 1951). A comparison of figures on a basis of young people of school age would be even more disadvantageous.

Most Latin educators with whom I talked agreed on two propositions: first, that a huge program of education is urgently needed in Latin America; and secondly, that far more than is now contemplated should be quickly inaugurated to launch such a program. In the teeth of the obvious need, the only intergovernmental effort I was able to find in the field of formal education was the $2,000,000 budgeted by the Organization of American States for 1960, and the $5,000,000 a year disposed of by the education division of the International Cooperation Administration—the U.S. Point Four Program.

With the accelerating rate of population growth in Latin America—and the growing Communist threat—tomorrow seems to me to be already yesterday in the field of education more than in any other.

Augusto Federico Schmidt, the Brazilian businessman-philosopher whom I have quoted before, told us that the magic phrases in Latin America are "economic development" and "social justice." But is it not obvious that the only open sesame to either is "education"? If there is any key to the future that is most hopeful, magic or otherwise, it is education.

I heard it argued in Latin America that if priorities must be established between economic development and education, economic development must come first—and literacy and education will follow; "the drive for mass literacy should not be allowed to hold up economic advance." Further, it was argued, priorities within education should go to production of "technically competent people," and should be "concentrated to fill areas of urgent need and strategic utility."

My own belief is that human beings are the greatest material resource of any nation, and their development is the first priority, even from a narrow economic viewpoint. An unpublished report

Table IV.–Education

Country	Population (1959–60)	Schools (1957–59) Primary	Enrollment	Secondary *	Enrollment *	Higher	Enrollment	% of pop. age 5 to 19 enrolled in school †	% of adult pop. without education ‡
Argentina	20,959,100	17,920	2,859,827	4,821	776,255	141	149,756	49	38
Bolivia	3,416,000	640	216,831	130	52,200	...	...	28	84
Brazil	66,302,271	82,953	5,775,246	5,635	1,023,897	764	84,481	..	79
Chile	7,551,000	6,886	1,011,429	389	163,559	29	11,405	52	23
Colombia	14,131,660	20,990	1,793,248	829	115,041	158	19,212	56	72
Costa Rica	1,125,828	1,416	165,666	78	29,559	1	3,111	43	62
Cuba	6,743,000	18,419	701,652	...	70,151	4	24,273	41	53
Dominican Republic	4,070,108	5,190	519,223	57	19,945	1	4,098	23	89
Ecuador	4,298,449	4,838	520,422	144	48,253	7	6,451	67	72
El Salvador	2,613,000	2,334	262,477	346	29,164	4	2,886	41	87
Guatemala	3,759,000	3,743	270,140	164	23,535	1	3,244	18	88
Haiti	3,505,000	1,500	199,115	53	20,857	1	982	..	93
Honduras	1,950,000	2,417	146,551	50	11,740	1	1,137	49	88
Mexico	34,625,903	29,263	4,110,853	2,022	332,106	26	293,000 (est.)	30	46
Nicaragua	1,450,349	1,983	118,679	362	7,561	2	916	20	84
Panama	1,053,000	1,155	142,576	88	30,936	1	2,454	62	55
Paraguay	1,728,292	2,040	289,952	117	23,662	1	2,982	60	79
Peru	10,857,000	12,944	1,233,937	606	138,796	9	21,273	..	..
Uruguay	2,800,000	...	301,596	121	70,876	1	16,000	..	..
Venezuela	6,709,000	6,791	735,111	460	83,493	5	10,553	51	77

* Generally includes vocational, technical and teacher-training schools. † Most data reflect the period about 1950 (most recent census); some data are estimates based on latest appraisals. ‡ In general includes those persons age 25 and over with less than four years of formal schooling and illiterates, and reflects the period about 1950.

prepared for the Organization of American States puts the issue succinctly:

> Of the factors that enter into the building of strong national economies, the most essential is trained personnel. In fact, it is the only indispensable factor. If good plans and programs for development projects do not exist, one can improvise. If capital is not available in adequate amounts, one can proceed more slowly and practice rigid economy. But if trained personnel are not available, it is idle to speak of national economic growth. . . . Even the will to initiate new activities, and the determination to promote national improvement, will arise and grow only in trained and educated minds.

In a growing population, illiterate and uneducated people add to the total of hunger and want; with education they become a "natural resource." It is my judgment that no broad program of economic development can succeed for long—no matter how much capital is poured into an economy, no matter how skillful the economic planning—unless it is accompanied by a program of education. New tools demand new men to control their use and to enjoy their fruits. Further, the good we seek in human affairs cannot be solely economic. Economic development is only one part of the general process of social development, and an overemphasis on the material aspects can lead to self-destructive twisting of the whole complicated web of personal and institutional relationships. Only through education can millions of Latin-Americans even begin to comprehend the part they can take in their awakening societies. Only through education can millions take the first steps of their upward climb not only to a better standard of living but also to a more decent, dignified view of the value of life. Further, only through education can trained and responsible political and business leaders be developed in sufficient numbers—leaders to guide the struggle for free democratic societies and for social equity, leaders to give human meaning to the technological revolution through which Latin America is beginning to pass.

Literacy and the Primary Schools

An estimated 70,000,000 to 80,000,000 of Latin America's peoples can neither read nor write. About half of these are more than 15 years old. The range of illiteracy percentages among those over age 10 runs from 13% for Argentina to 89% for Haiti, with huge Brazil listed at 51%.

Latin America's primary schools are inadequate, to use a mild adjective. They have little equipment and few books. Frequently teachers work only part time and are equipped with only elementary school education themselves. The subject matter is antiquated.

The feudal way of life that still persists in much of Latin America has not been conducive to large-scale education. The oligarchic tradition may have given and may still give a relatively small elite an education fitting their self-conceived aristocratic roles, but the great masses of the people are receiving little if any education and this little of poor quality. The present task of providing a public-school system adequate to the needs is thus monumental.

Vittorino Veronese, Director-General of the UN Educational, Scientific and Cultural Organization (UNESCO) which has studied the problem, reached the reasonable conclusion that in Latin America, "we must begin at the beginning." He suggested that Latin America needs 500,000 more primary teachers and as many classrooms if it is to make primary education available for the 19,000,000 children who have yet to begin their education. UNESCO itself is not set up to direct such a task. It has only a limited budget available for "fundamental education." It can hope only to provide modest leadership, through surveys and pilot projects.

The individual Latin-American countries vary greatly in literacy. Costa Rica proudly declares that it has more school-teachers than soldiers. This helps account for a literacy rate of almost 80%, a figure Costa Rica shares with Argentina, Chile and Uruguay. At the opposite end, in Bolivia, Guatemala and Honduras, the literate comprise only 30% and in Haiti only 11%. All these figures are necessarily inexact. Usually the "literate" include all those who have received any formal schooling. Since most educators agree that four years of schooling are usually necessary to create any lasting degree of literacy, the number of people who are "functionally illiterate" in Latin America is probably far greater than the 70,000,000 to 80,000,000 admitted. The situation is roughly comparable to that in Russia when the Bolsheviks seized power in 1917.

Compounding the whole problem of education is the current population bulge. The proportion of children to adults is growing greater. In Venezuela, for example, 70% of the population is under 30 years of age. For Latin America as a whole, the proportion of children of school age to adults is twice what it is in Europe. Thus the burden of education is potentially twice as heavy on each adult worker. And this burden is the more onerous because so many people are hungry, and because they need money for new roads, for new hospitals and new housing as well as new schools.

A major extra difficulty confronting educators in the so-called "Indian countries" is language. In these countries the children speak their own native Indian languages. Many learn no Spanish, even in families where the father has acquired a working knowledge of it. This language barrier is far more formidable than I had suspected. It calls for the difficult training of bilingual teachers and the preparation of bilingual textbooks. Further required is an expensive program of missionary work to persuade the Indian fathers to keep their children in school.

THE MEXICAN PROGRAM.—Let me take Mexico as a sample of the latter problem and of others. Mexico's mass education movement grew out of its great revolution of 1910. (The Mexicans say with regret that most of their neighbors to the south "haven't yet had their revolutions!") This socially well-adjusted country prides itself on its understanding of the role education must play. In contrast to only 7% of its federal budget devoted to its armed services, it allocates 17½% to education. Further, we were told that some of the individual Mexican states are spending more than 50% of their budgets on education.

Despite nearly 40 years of effort to bring schools to the most isolated villages, in 1950 (the latest national census figure available when this was written) about 38% of the Mexican people did not have any formal education. Further, according to 1956 estimates, of every 1,000 children who began school, 866 dropped out before the completion of the primary grades and more than half by the end of the first year. (The Indian fathers often feel the child is needed to help out at home.) Only 59 of the 1,000, or about 6%, entered the secondary schools, and more than half of these quit before completion. Just 6 of the original 1,000 enrolled in a university, and 5 of these dropped out at some point during the four- to six-year course. This left only 1 in 1,000 who eventually received a university degree. One reason for the high dropout is the failure of the schools to offer the technical training which is in such demand by industry.

Jaime Torres Bodet is Mexico's present Minister of Education. He is a former Minister of Foreign Affairs, former Director-General of UNESCO, a distinguished poet and an extremely intelligent and charming man with a well-deserved international reputation as an educator. He proposes to change the foregoing statistics. He is an old hand at combating Mexican illiteracy. He fostered a country-wide campaign in 1944 while previously serving as minister of education. He then called on every Mexican who could read to teach one other Mexican who could not. This was adult education on a national scale that electrified the country. Torres Bodet told us that this had worked successfully for about three or four years, but then "the initial enthusiasm had declined." (I suspect that this decline in enthusiasm may have been due to Torres Bodet's shift to the foreign ministry and his later move to UNESCO in Paris.) Today his emphasis has switched. It is now on formal primary education, the first six grades. In the rural areas of Mexico, he told us, there are often only three grades, and he intends to build them up, adding a grade at a time. There are now 4,100,000 children in Mexico's primary schools, and within

11 years he hopes to step this figure up to 7,200,000. This, he hopes, would bring Mexico close to the proportion of U.S. youngsters now in primary schools. However, one of the problems is that the population of Mexico may easily reach a net increase of more than 3% a year.

Torres Bodet refers to this as an "11-year primary education plan." He described it as a "very big and costly program." Mexico's 1959 federal budget now allots 1,500,000,000 pesos to his ministry of education. Over the 11-year span the new program will require an additional 4,800,000,000 pesos and 70,000 new teachers. (This represents an "extraordinary" expenditure, in addition to the "ordinary" budget of the ministry of education, which increases by about 18% every year, and it will only apply to the expansion of primary education.)

"It is not always easy to obtain the funds we need for education," reported Torres Bodet, thus echoing the complaint of educators the world over. He continued, "When President Avila Camacho was in office, I recall the high priority he gave to road building. He felt that rural education must start with roads. To him, the road was a school which moves." And Torres Bodet agrees that roads have to be built into inaccessible areas to facilitate the task of teachers and the work of schools.

Torres Bodet showed us samples of the free textbooks he is only now beginning to make available at government expense to the first four grades. Hitherto the existing textbooks were expensive and consequently not within the reach of every parent. Further, Torres Bodet plans extensive use of filmstrips. Whereas in the U.S. our teachers often prefer motion pictures, he feels the filmstrips, which are motionless pictures in sequence, are better for the elementary teachers. He thinks that filmstrips are very practical because they can be accompanied with the teacher's explanations, and because of the fact that they can be easily shown as many times as necessary. (In Brazil, we were told that neither motion pictures nor filmstrips could be widely used because of the lack of electric power in the rural elementary schools.)

In February 1960, when we called upon him, Torres Bodet told us that a recent decision established a requirement under which anyone seeking a teacher's certificate must first devote a year to teaching in rural or small-town schools. (Everywhere in Latin America the large cities attract concentrations of the best professional talent—talent which seems unwilling to go to outlying

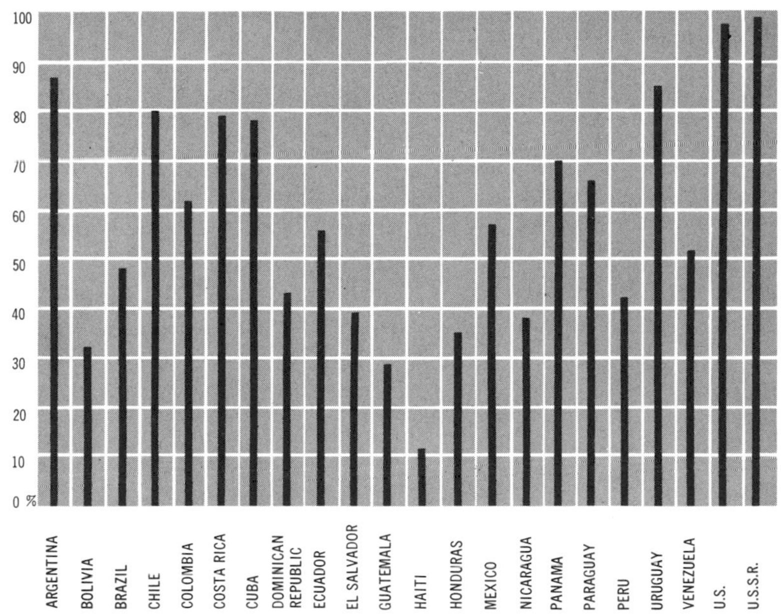

Literacy rate of countries of Latin America, U.S. and U.S.S.R. showing percentage of population 15 years of age or older able to read and write. (*Sources:* UNESCO, U.S.S.R. Embassy press release)

areas.) Such service is also required of Mexican doctors. Torres Bodet would pay his novice teachers the same beginning salaries they would receive in the cities. He hoped that many would decide they liked the country, would find that the salary went much further and would settle down to country life. The opposition to this decision among teacher-trainees at the National Teacher School in Mexico City was so great that a few weeks after we left Mexico, when the plan was announced, the students rioted and went on strike against it.

> (Harold F. Clark of Teachers College, Columbia, tells me that "it has been fairly well demonstrated in most countries of the world that it is extremely difficult to have a teacher train in a large city and expect him to go back to the village. . . . In almost all cases the training institution should be located in a small, agricultural community. . . . At least in the early stages of the program, the periods of training may have to be kept quite short. . . .")

I asked Torres Bodet how a child in a rural area who had learned to read might keep up with his reading after leaving school. Without books in his home or available in a library, how can he avoid slipping back into illiteracy? The minister explained that "little reading rooms for mass reading" are to be installed in conjunction with rural schools. Ideally, these will contain 50 or 60 books keyed to the interests of the community—such as books on agricultural improvement. Here people of all ages may gather and read aloud in groups. Such centers and such materials are among Latin America's most urgent needs.

Governor Stevenson asked the minister whether the continuing migration to the cities was leaving the Indian isolated in the rural areas. (Mexico City has grown from 1,000,000 to 2,700,000 in 25 years and the Federal District, of which it is the center, to nearly 5,000,000.) Torres Bodet agreed that this was a problem. He then told us of the remarkable work of Alfonso Caso, an anthropologist devoted to the Indian people, through his National Indian Institute. The Institute and his co-ordinating centers should help keep the Indian on the land. There are now 8 such centers with 16 more in preparation. They give courses in Spanish; they offer technical assistance for the improvement of agriculture and the arts; they provide engineers to help develop irrigation and other improvements. They are autonomous but require government money to operate.

Mexico, a relatively advanced country, illustrates the depth of the literacy problem. If the objective is to reduce illiteracy drastically in a short time, the schools by themselves cannot do the job. They will take a generation or possibly two. Thus, other means are also needed such as Torres Bodet's movement of the 40s—plus the widespread use of the radio which should be inaugurated on a vast scale at once as the only medium that can reach into every hamlet. Further, after literacy has reached 60% or more, let us say, the national effort should probably be re-oriented toward training in agricultural efficiency. Indeed, the two go hand in hand. One reason the peon or poor farmer will want to learn to read is so that he can learn how to produce more food.

Brazil provides another example of the difficulties at the elementary level. In Rio de Janeiro, Brazil's then Deputy Minister of Education, Anísio Espínola Teixeira, explained to me that in 1930 there were only 1,800,000 students in Brazil's elementary schools. Now there are 5,800,000. But he said there would be 7,500,000 if all Brazilian youngsters from 7 to 11 were in school.

Teixeira told me that most of the elementary schools have no books. They desperately need "a much higher priority on books." And he added that reference books were the most important of all books needed. I feel that the educational advancement of the children and the people of Brazil is one of the great goals and one of the great philanthropic opportunities of the western world. Brazil is the emerging giant of the southern hemisphere.

After the books, says Teixeira, comes teacher training. Only 2,800,000 or about one half of the 5,800,000 students have teachers who have ever attended secondary school; 3,000,000 have teachers with only primary training. The great expansion of students has resulted in "deteriorated standards for teachers."

Brigadier José Vicente de Faria Lima, the state of São Paulo's Minister of Public Works, explained to us that the shortage of classrooms in the state of São Paulo calls for new primary rooms to accommodate 320,000 students on two new shifts, plus the replacement of old and obsolete primary rooms which will take care of another 240,000 students on two shifts. The new primary schools will be wired for electricity, and there are plans for the use of filmstrips but none as yet for motion pictures or television.

In addition, new secondary schools must be built in São Paulo for 110,000 students, plus 30 new professional schools for 7,200 students. (The state is now carrying the whole cost for this program but is trying to get federal aid.)

The state of São Paulo is by far the richest of Brazil's 20 states and 6 territories. It contributes 41% of all Brazil's governmental receipts. If its education needs are so acute—if it finds it necessary to plan an educational program geared to two shifts of students—this will help give some idea of the tragic shortages throughout the rest of Brazil.

COLOMBIA.—Gov. Alberto Jaramillo, of the state of Antioquia, Colombia, told us that there are 8,000 children in Medellín—a rich city of 500,000 population which boasts 100 or more millionaires—who cannot go to school because there are no facilities. He said that the city is supposed to build the schoolhouses; the state is supposed to pay the teachers; and the federal government helps in various ways. The Governor explained that the money problem is very tough for the states because "congress takes any new revenues for the federal government." This is a good example of a chronic problem affecting the relationship between provincial governments and the central government throughout the hemisphere.

TEACHING ADULTS TO READ.—Not all Latin-American educators agree with Torres Bodet's emphasis on the primary role of formal schooling among today's educational needs. Alberto Giesecke, former Rector of the University of Cuzco in Peru, who is now working with the U.S. Embassy in Lima, feels that priority should be given to a literacy program for adults. He told us that such a program could achieve important results with the Indians within ten years. However, I am told that most students of comparative education agree with Torres Bodet; they argue that experience around the world shows that adult literacy programs tend to be ineffective except where a good elementary school program is operating.

In Bogotá we heard about a remarkable priest named Monsignor Salcedo. He is widely known as "the good monsignor." He

Credit: Alberto Tardio

Indian women and children learning to read at a rural school in Bolivia.

teaches the illiterate to read by radio, and his program has been described as "one of the most dramatic campaigns to overcome illiteracy in all the world." His audience is estimated at 500,000. He gets someone in each village who knows how to read to act as the leader of a group that works together under the guidance of his broadcasts; there are 6,500 such groups. One of his broadcast series deals with agriculture—how to take care of the cows, how to get better seeds and the like. In addition, he has a weekly newspaper, dealing largely with agriculture, which has a circulation of 75,000, almost the circulation of the big Bogotá daily *El Tiempo*. (A somewhat similar program, also successful, was started in Bolivia by Father Ryan in 1956.)

Monsignor Salcedo, recently chosen "UN Man of the Year," is subsidized by the Colombian government. When an anticlerical group went to President Lleras Camargo and demanded that his subsidy be cut off, the president refused. He said, "Come and see me when you have a proposal that will promise to do the country as much good with the same amount of money."

I do not feel the argument about combating illiteracy should be allowed to narrow to that of "primary school *v.* adult education." The case for greatly expanded elementary education is overwhelming and cannot be denied. But surely there are also outstanding opportunities in the field of teaching adults, particularly through the great new media of radio and television. Monsignor Salcedo offers an example which should be followed—and not resisted. And Giesecke may be right. The race with the Communists over the next decade, applied to the Indians, may be primarily at the level of adult education. Indeed, broadcasting may provide the best hope for educational progress in rural Latin America during the years that will be required to enlarge the teaching force and develop the schools. Receivers could be installed relatively quickly in every village and the broadcasts could be aimed not only toward increasing literary but toward providing community education in agriculture, sanitation, the improvement of homes and also toward an effort to do something about formal elementary education.

Secondary Schools

I have already touched upon the first crucial point in any discussion of public secondary education. This is the "desertion rate." The greatest incidence occurs after the first year of primary school. The second is between the primary and the secondary school. A major reason for the latter is that there are insufficient vocational schools at the secondary level. Thus, secondary schooling now largely means a commitment either to eventual university training or to shabby gentility in such white collar occupations as rural schoolteaching or bookkeeping. It is not too tempting. The students turn away.

Very few secondary schools of any kind are in operation in the rural sections. This deprives country people of the education essential to their chances to move up. One consequence is that migration to the city takes place most often among undertrained persons, and the slum settlements get bigger and more destitute.

The secondary schools in the urban areas suffer from lack of money, from frequent turnover of teachers and from outdated courses. Quite a few are on two and three shifts a day. Many of the teachers are university students who teach only part time. Colombia's President Lleras Camargo told us that "there are now over a million Colombians who should be in secondary schools and are not; those who are there are studying the same courses as in the 19th century."

The antiquated curricula weaken the ability of the universities, in turn, to impose a modern content on their own curricula. The youngsters from wealthier families can, of course, avail themselves of well-run private schools. Thus—and this point is important—the failure to fill the gap between primary and university training with reasonably good public secondary instruction serves to harden class distinctions. This is dangerous as well as unjust. Unless "social mobility" increases at the educational level—unless the newly ambitious submerged classes find the opportunity to move higher—Latin America's "impatience" can more readily turn into violence.

In Brazil, many public secondary schools operate on three shifts—morning, afternoon and evening. Federico Rangel, in Brazil's ministry of education, told me that the instruction is so weak that Brazil's seven engineering schools can't find enough qualified students to keep up with Brazil's economy which is currently rushing ahead in productivity at a rate of increase of 7% or 8% a year. This is a critical part of the acute present problem in Brazil; how can the country, with such a woefully weak educational system, sustain its rapid economic growth?

Private Schools

The private primary and secondary schools are usually the best. They are largely run for families who can afford to pay the tuition. Frequently they are conducted by the Catholic Church. There are many, notably in the capitals, which receive the encouragement and support of foreign governments. Traditionally, for example, the French and Germans have sponsored such schools, and not merely for the children of their own nationals. If wellborn Latin-American youngsters are taught French or German—or English—this, it is argued, will help cement the ties that bind. This will pay off in long range diplomatic and commercial terms.

In Quito, Governor Stevenson and I were fortunate to spend a morning at the American school. It charges a tuition fee of $14 a month. This is more than the national per capita income of about $13 a month. Galo Plaza, who served a four-year term (1948–1952) as president of Ecuador, helped to found this school in 1940. Plaza, who had been educated in the United States, wanted a school to combat the Axis propaganda emanating from the Quito German school. Now chairman of the board of trustees of the American school, Plaza told us that the school has about 800 students, from kindergarten through high school, of whom only 60 are U.S. nationals. There is also a U.S. missionary school in Quito with 125 to 150 students, all U.S. nationals; and two Catholic schools, one for boys and one for girls, both named after Cardinal Spellman and sponsored by him. (The German school, closed after Pearl Harbor, has reopened and is prospering once more.)

Plaza's American school receives Quaker support. It provides a number of scholarships. Many have been given to full-blooded Indians who have later done well in the United States in our universities. Plaza told us of three Indian brothers, all of whom have received scholarships at the school and later at U.S. universities. The four grandparents of these boys are full-blooded Indian peasant farmers. One grandson secured a scholarship at Princeton and graduated *magna cum laude;* he was then given $2,000 for a graduate fellowship to study philosophy at Harvard, but decided that Harvard's philosophy department had gone to pieces after George Santayana's retirement; he turned in his $2,000 and is now at the Sorbonne in Paris. The second is a top athlete earning scholastic honors at the University of Texas. The third is preparing himself for a career as a concert pianist. Plaza told us this story as an answer to the arguments of those who say it is a waste of time to try to educate the Indians. The whole history of Indians in this American school denies the racist theory that there is any inherent intellectual superiority in the white races.

The principal of the school, Robert Cornish, with an M.A. from the University of Iowa, proudly told us that all the youngsters graduate "friendly to the United States" and remain so.

Not too long ago in Latin America the girls and boys, at school and elsewhere, were kept strictly and widely separated. They still are at the Cardinal Spellman schools, as indeed they are in parochial secondary schools in the U.S. Plaza told us that only in this century have Latin-American women begun to achieve acceptance in a man's world. The progress in Ecuador has been remarkable. Plaza regards this American school as a symbol. The school divides about equally between boys and girls. We saw those of the second grade dancing together, and thought them delightful and amusing. They were performing native Ecuadorian dances in which the girl uses the handkerchief to cover her face and eyes, in the manner of the old Spanish "flirtation dance." Here at this school is coeducation in the old Quaker tradition—though the Quakers were never dancers!

Schools of comparable quality are unhappily far too few. Until they become more numerous, at the public level as well as the private—and thus available to children from the poorest families—college and university education in Latin America will languish for lack of trained applicants.

Meanwhile, an encouraging development is the aid being given by the U.S. government to 200 Latin secondary schools through the Inter-American Schools service maintained by the American Council on Education.

Hardly anyone in Latin America emphasizes the necessity for keeping the educational stream of trained and talented young people flowing from kindergarten all the way through to the graduate and professional school. This, however, is a major part not only of the educational but of the democratic process. It is the heart of Latin America's educational problem. It requires not only vastly expanded primary and secondary education but a quality of public education that will permit the institutions of higher education to flourish. In the latter, the future leadership must largely be trained.

Higher Education and the Universities

Perhaps the single most revealing remark made to me in Latin America about higher education was made by Nabor Carrillo, the Rector of the National University of Mexico. Almost casually, he said that while he himself had held office for 7 years, his 11 predecessors had had an average tenure of 1 year and 10 months—and three of them had resigned under imminent danger of physical violence.

There are only about 120 universities—the exact number depends on how one classifies universities—in the 20 republics of Latin America; of these, more than 100 are national universities.

Their enrollment totals approximately 430,000. A great majority of these institutions, many of them of most ancient lineage, have wholly failed to keep pace with today's world standards. They are hampered by underpaid and part-time professors whose main interests lie elsewhere; by political interference; by grossly inadequate budgets and administrative machinery; and by a degree of student control not conceivable to parents and educators in Europe and the United States. Some, such as the University of Buenos Aires, with more than 60,000 students, are among the largest in the world. Others are small and still others seem to be yet in the planning stages. The national universities in Mexico City and Caracas are splendidly housed on supercampuses called "university cities." Such campuses are now planned for Brazil's leading university and for the University of Buenos Aires. But most are inadequately housed in old buildings strewn here and there throughout their cities.

The ultramodern buildings of the National University of Mexico were financed during the administration of Pres. Miguel Alemán, a gigantic statue of whom towers over the campus. They were built in the 1950s at a cost of $30,000,000. The result, in bricks and mortar, is perhaps roughly equivalent to a $100,000,000 investment in the United States.

Such a "university city," removed from the center of the city, may seem too grandiose to some but it can give to progressive rectors and deans a new chance. Such a central suburban campus invites the adoption of the U.S. departmental system, which in turn requires full-time teachers. Further, political manipulation is harder in the suburbs than in the city. Floaters and aging "professional" students are discouraged by the distance from the city center.

In Caracas, as we passed a gigantic and beautiful new building, I asked our guide, Señora Pérez, "Is this the university?" She replied, "It is the ministry of defense—what else?" Later we passed a huge library built for the university but, according to Señora Pérez, "it has no books." (In the corrupt Pérez Jiménez dictatorship of 1953–1958 an easy way to steal from the public purse was through so-called public works, from which the politicians are said to have extracted a "take" of up to 40%.)

Thus, great differences exist among the universities and among the schools within them—in entrance requirements, in standards for degrees, in quality of faculties and in the support they receive from their governments. Some of the independent faculties will not recognize the students or credits of other faculties within the same university. Tuition is low in all national universities; for example, $7 a year at Peru's ancient University of San Marco and $16 a year at the National University of Mexico.

University Organization and Some of Its Consequences.—There is, however, one organic similarity among them all. They share a system of academic organization and control which resembles that which developed in Bologna in Italy around the beginning of the 13th century. In Europe at that time there were two main types of university organization—that of Paris and that of Bologna. The Paris type was a corporation of scholars (or masters) who operated the university; they made and enforced the rules and opposed even the king or papal legate when they thought that the rights of the university were threatened. Indeed, if the scholars feared persecution, they would pick up and move the university, like an Arab with his tents, camels, wives and followers. Bologna, by contrast, was a corporation of students. There the students engaged the professors, set the terms of their contracts and reminded them in various ways that they were the hired men.

Institutions of the Bologna type were relatively short lived in Italy, and all universities in Europe and the United States today are descendants of Paris or Paris-plan institutions. In their direction the students have little or no say. Typically, in U.S. universities an academic council or senate composed of senior professors and deans is responsible for the development of the curriculum and for academic standards. A board of trustees, composed of laymen, is charged with over-all policy. (This lay board of trustees is the United States' unique contribution to university organization and although it often includes older—and conservative!—alumni, the students themselves have no voice in its control.)

In contrast, all Latin-American national universities (with exceptions in Brazil where students "make representations" and go on strike but do not sit on the governing councils) have an organization and administration resembling the old Bologna model. Some observers believe the recrudescence of the Bologna type may be characteristic of underdeveloped countries, where economic and social conditions make it relatively easy to transform large groups of young people into political instruments.

Now and again a Latin-American university may acquire a special stamp from a national dictator who exercises direct control over its academic life. Or a species of direct governmental control may occasionally crop up in the form of legal proscriptions and decrees. But leaving such nuances aside, the common characteristic remains the Bologna-type organization. On the ruling councils sit student representatives, often in such numbers as to make effective faculty control of curriculums and discipline exceedingly difficult if not impossible.

At Central University in Quito we were told that the university council—the governing body—consists of the rector, the vice-rector, a representative of the ministry of education, the nine deans of the schools or divisions of the university and nine students. Governor Stevenson told a group of students in Quito: "I used to think as a student I'd like to run the university but later on in life I decided that I was wrong."

In Mexico City, Rector Carrillo described to me how his university is organized. On the council responsible for its control are 16 deans from the various schools and divisions. One professor and one elected student from each school or division are also chosen. To these are added the 20 directors of the research institutes. At the meetings the 16 students are entitled to bring 16 alternates.

The council elects a 15-man board of governors, passes on the selection of the rector, on the appointment of the professors and on the curriculum itself. Indeed it reviews each detail of university administration except budgetary matters. For these the council elects three trustees. Elected for life, these trustees have sole responsibility for the budget and the money. However, they have nothing to do with the curriculum or the conduct of the university—except the money.

STUDENT INFLUENCE AND CONTROL.—The heavy student representation on the ruling bodies seems to be a mechanism for anarchy built into the Latin-American system of higher education. This of course would not produce such extreme results if it were not for highly unstable political environments.

There is always the unspoken threat of a student strike or student violence if the student opinion on the council does not get its way. Further, standards set under student pressure are often very low. This arrangement well serves the so-called "professional students"—the perpetual students who often stay on until they are well into their 30's because they find that the university connection helps them get easy jobs and helps them achieve celebrity as leaders of student political agitation which is in turn a steppingstone to a career in law or politics. Because such career students tend to come from middle- and upper-bracket families, and because politics is still quite oligarchical and classbound, they have a high expectation of promotion into leading roles in politics. As students, they feel they are merely starting young on what is a preordained course, given the nature of the social structure.

Unhappily few students can be flunked out. Often the students enforce a policy of low standards upon the professors. A frequent student slogan has been, "Never let a student fail!" Even students who pass their courses have gone on strike to force professors to pass failing students. They have also struck because a course is too difficult or to force a professor to change the course.

Such student participation in university administration springs in part from the view that the function of the university is to take a direct and immediate role in active political life. The Latin university thus lacks protection from the buffetings of politics. Indeed, the students tear down the walls of protection from the inside, and public affairs then press in unhindered on the affairs of the classroom. The freedom of expression and contemplation and experimentation–free of immediate consequence –necessary for true academic freedom as this is understood in Europe and the U.S., are only uncommonly found in Latin-American higher education. The students themselves thereby pay a very high price. For their privilege of manipulating power which they are not equipped to exercise or even understand, they risk losing the kind of education that would qualify them as leaders of that very social improvement which some of them think they seek to promote.

What kind of young people are these students? The argument is made that the low tuition charges are democratic, allowing anyone a college education. The truth of the matter seems to be the opposite: by and large only the better-off families can afford to send their children to secondary school, or better yet to private school, where they can prepare for the university–or can afford to support them long enough to complete a college education. There are of course some exceptions; only about 2% of the students in the University of Buenos Aires come from working-class families. The percentage seems to be even lower in countries such as Guatemala. The university, then, in practice stamps lines of class division deep into society, lines which took form far down in the educational process.

Many students feel that the fact that they have a college education means that society thereafter owes them a permanent special status. But because they often receive no real or significant training, there develops a group of displaced (or better, never-placed) persons who are theoretically schooled but not trained, and who find society unable to absorb them. They are picturesquely called the "intellectual proletariat." They are a politically dangerous and often highly irresponsible group. Unable to make a go of it in the field in which they originally start, as perennial students they enroll in another and start all over again. (Because in many institutions a student cannot transfer credits earned in one "faculty" to another one, he must indeed start all over. The mathematics or the sociology taught in humanities is "different," so far as the student is concerned, from the mathematics or sociology taught, say, in economics. This can keep a student going indefinitely.) One of the great needs in Latin-American higher education, to which the U.S. might contribute through its technical assistance program, is some planning which will cut down on the surplus of people who concentrate in a few fields such as law—and divert students into courses which are developed to help meet the economy's critical personnel shortages. The universities today are largely geared to students who seek to specialize in law, medicine or government service. They have not adjusted themselves to the emerging industrial societies.

One Argentine professor of physics spoke to me with particular passion. He said that of the 60,000 students in his University of Buenos Aires there were only "two or three good workers." (This I took to be an exaggeration for purposes of emphasis—in any assemblage of young people a substantial proportion will be earnest students.) During his youth at a European and then at a U.S. university, he recalled, "Many of the students were so poor they could only get their hair cut once every three months—but they attended classes and they worked!" Then with a sweeping gesture to take in his immediate environment he exclaimed: "These Argentinian children are being trained to become parasites and to take over the government. The students almost invariably become the 'smart boys' who feel the world owes them a living." Worse still, he said, with no compulsory attendance and with standards so low, it is impossible for him to get rid of students who are worthless. "I have just failed one student for the sixth time," he concluded, "and I expect him to enroll again." [2]

[2] A "census" of the University of Buenos Aires, taken in the autumn of 1958 and made available after our departure, helps place these statements in perspective. Here are some facts drawn from the "census": Total number of students 58,684, 90% under 30 years of age. One third of all students (*i.e.*, 20,000) drop out after one year of study (in law the corresponding figure is

A professor of the social sciences who was with us took a brighter view. He pointed out that 2,000 of the 60,000 students were teaching in the primary grades. "That takes work," he said. With this the physics professor reluctantly agreed, adding hastily, "These are the best students." He then expressed the conviction that the education job cannot ever be done by the national universities for "too much politics makes the students' lot too easy." He is seeking support for the founding of a private university, where students will not dominate the faculty and curriculum.

COMMUNIST STUDENTS.—Many of the "professional students" have direct connections with the various national political parties and live on political subsidies. In this group are many hard-core Communists, trained to manipulate a 5% or 10% following in the student body which could tip the political balance of the entire student corps.

In Montevideo, we were told, the student political activities are Communist controlled; in Caracas the Communists also ma-

---

49%). Less than 30% of all students attend classes regularly (reason for this given by students themselves: "We have to work to support ourselves"). Only 36% of all students do not have jobs (although in prestige fields, such as medicine and dentistry, these are 52% and 58%). Expressed the other way around, 64% of the students have jobs, a third of these in work unconnected with their studies. Although 72% live with their families, only 30% are supported by their families (this is roughly the 36% who do not work). The enrollment in the main faculties of the University of Buenos Aires in the autumn of 1958, is reported as follows:

	Students enrolled	*% Total students*
Medicine	14,986	25.5
Law	10,849	18.6
Economic sciences (90% Accounting) (10% Economics)	10,329	17.6
Engineering	7,186	12.2
Pharmacy and Biochemistry	2,695	4.6
Exact sciences	1,891	3.2
Agronomy and veterinary medicine	1,219	2.1

nipulate effectively. At the National University of Mexico, I was informed that only 5% of the students really qualify as "radical leftists" or Communists. I pointed out to my informant that this was a smashing 2,500 students, quite enough to start a large-scale riot.

Of course, participation in politics is a birthright of Latin-American students, handed down from their forebears. Because of the general respect shown the intellectual in Latin America, and because in a few countries a significantly increasing number of students come from the middle and lower middle classes and are impatient for social reform, the students have a weight and purpose in their political activities unknown in the U.S. They are feeling a strong pull to the Communist party which lavishes its attentions upon them.

The Plight of the Professors.—In Latin America as a whole professorial salaries are well under those that qualified men earn in other careers. They range from a low of about $40 a month for part-time professors (who are often interested primarily in building prestige in their professions) to $200 or at most $300 a month for full time. Many part-time professors, and such part-time experts will be needed for at least another generation, have been carelessly selected, and are so-called "taxi" professors who, when they do not send unqualified substitutes to do the teaching, use "warmed up notes from courses they once took in Europe." But many of the full-time professors we met seemed dedicated men. A number of them knew that I myself had been sitting on a mourner's bench because of the shortcomings of the U.S. educational system. Since they had no reason to expect from me a patronizing lecture—that of a Yankee blind to the weaknesses of education in his own country—they were, I believe, the more candid with me. (I was warned that I might have to discount what leading Latin-American professors say about Latin-American students because the two groups are in open competition—and the professors feel threatened by the students.)

In Chile an economist of international fame confirmed what I learned in Mexico and the Argentine: that professors were poorly prepared, frequently absent and constantly being changed; that classes were enormous and the chief role of the professor was to give examinations. Further, he said, the "student rule" demoralized the universities. There was little incentive for a student to study in an effort to pass. In Chile as in Argentina, a student could fail his courses one month and start all over again the next. This in itself would discourage any professor.

SOME HOPEFUL PROGRESS.—Leading Latin-American scholars themselves acknowledge that their universities suffer from low academic standards induced in part by inept organization. Rector Frondizi, shortly after taking office at the University of Buenos Aires, wrote an article for *Comentario*, in which he said, in part:

> . . . The Argentine university has wasted much of its energies in the search for ingenious solutions to administrative questions, without becoming aware that the problems of the university are of a pedagogical nature . . . that instruction should be scarce or nonexistent has seemed of little importance. Nor does it matter that the university does no research, that one turns one's back on the necessities of the country, that there are no professors fit to teach many courses, that the students still keep on repeating by memory the used-up notes of previous years, that the professors themselves repeat those same notes and demand them back in the examinations, that there is no university life, that the degree is the principal goal . . . and the examination the immediate objective.

This article caused a sensation when it appeared, especially because Frondizi went on to suggest remedies: improvement in teaching techniques; the importation of foreign scholars where necessary; scholarships for study in Argentina and abroad; the training of more veterinarians, for example, and fewer lawyers; the building of libraries and laboratories; the establishment of departments within and among the colleges; and changes in course programs to allow for a number of optional courses instead of the stout lists of wholly required and often antiquated materials. Frondizi's article also included a round condemnation of grandiose so-called survey courses (he called them *cursos kilométricos*) and recommended a cutback in attempted instruction by straight lectures. Finally, he called for the establishment of the doctorate as a general prerequisite for faculty membership as is customary in Europe and the U.S.

Frondizi insists that under present conditions he prefers to have students on his university council. Through them, he feels that he has a chance to persuade the student agitators to accept his policies. "I'd much rather have the students inside listening and talking to me," he said, "than outside working against me." This may help show the deep-seated danger of the student threat —and the present need for compromise and concession in handling it in a sensitive political environment. It also seems clearly to illumine the acute administrative problem in operating a great urban state university.

Federico Pinedo of Argentina, onetime Minister of Finance and a former professor, told me that, because of the power of the left-wing student organizations over university affairs throughout Latin America, he once asked the Soviet ambassador to Argentina whether Soviet students were permitted to run the universities in the U.S.S.R. The ambassador snapped back, "Absolutely not!")

Rector Frondizi's brother, the president of Argentina, "has made the modernization of Argentine universities a major policy of his government," the *New York Times* reported after our return. And Rector Frondizi has made progress, very real progress. In the past four years the University of Buenos Aires has regained its autonomy; the number of full-time professors has been increased from 5 to more than 100; student scholarships have been established; U.S. foundations are now making grants to the university; a contract with Columbia University under the International Cooperation administration has been recently signed and impetus has been given to research in general.

Further, a start has been made toward instituting a departmental system patterned after that of U.S. universities; entrance examinations are now being given by many faculties and standards are inching up. A "self-study" has been under way for three years which is teaching the university many things about itself. But many negative influences remain: political dissension among the students and professors continues rampant; the threat of the loss of autonomy is constant; Catholics and anti-Catholics continue their battles about the control of higher education; there is not enough money; the plant continues dispersed; the libraries are shameful—and so forth!

In a wry way, Rector Carrillo told me that the National University of Mexico had lately begun to raise its standards. To deal with the problem of the "professional student," it is setting a limit on the number of times a student can fail. Under the present canon, a student can be dropped after failing ten subjects or failing one subject three times. The university's director of public relations excused the low standards by pointing out that so few young Mexicans ever reach the university at all, and that their preparation has been so poor, that the university must be lenient.

I would not wish to see an end to the goal of political and intellectual autonomy for Latin-American universities. Such autonomy grew through the centuries of struggle with the Spanish crown and clerical power. Later, the present key role of the students was triggered by the so-called Córdoba university reform of 1918 in which the students forced their way into the administration of the University of Córdoba, Argentina; this began as an uprising by serious students against the clique of professors who regarded their posts as sinecures. It spread throughout Latin America and is known as the "1918 Córdoba Revolution."

Nor do I undervalue the spirit of liberalism that brought students to the forefront of resistance to dictatorship in many lands. Often theirs has been almost the sole audible liberal voice. Indeed, the prestige which clings to the political activities of students in many countries is in part a legacy from the role they have played in helping pull down tyrants such as Perón and Batista.

The fate visited by the Castro regime on the University of Havana, 232-year-old citadel of Cuban culture with 22,000 students, is an example both of the loss of autonomy and the evils of student control. Before Castro, the university had achieved such autonomy that no Batista policeman dared set foot in its precincts. One of Castro's first moves as premier was to install 12 of his student followers on the university council. These new councilors at first moved for reforms that appeared to many to be legitimate. But soon they donned revolvers, began training an armed student militia and announced that the university must become "an instrument of the revolution." They in effect now control the institution. Thus far, more than 400 members of the 1,600-man faculty have been fired, many of them obviously because they lacked sufficient enthusiasm for Castroism. The professor of ancient history, in his lectures on Alexander, now compares the campaigns of Alexander with those of Fidel Castro. I like to hope that this latest and most tragic example of the dangers of student and political control may serve throughout the hemisphere to point up the urgent need for the autonomy and reform of the Latin-American universities.

Private Universities

One of the great needs of Latin America is for the establishment of private universities which can set standards. The establishment of church universities, which have been prohibited, has been argued for more than half a century in Argentina. President Frondizi, as part of his campaign promises, strengthened himself with the Catholic vote by promising a break in the monopoly of the state university system. He has made good on these promises. Under Argentina's new administration, the medical, legal, teaching and other diplomas of authorized private universities are to be recognized and thus will achieve legal status. Three private universities are already being organized by Catholic groups. In a private university, the faculty and administrators can more easily wrest control from the students and can seek to set up higher academic standards.

But the chances are remote that these private universities will achieve notably higher quality in the foreseeable future. They too will suffer from the general shortage of professors, the general lack of money and plant, the lack of an academic tradition and one of philanthropy. The new Catholic universities may decide to specialize—as, for example, in medicine at Córdoba—in which case their chances for quick and limited successes are quite good. Further, greater faculty control should reduce some of the more flagrant abuses of student domination.

THE UNIVERSITY OF THE ANDES.—High in the mountains of Colombia, in Bogotá, Governor Stevenson and I visited one of the most unusual—and promising—universities in Latin America. Founded only 12 years ago, the University of the Andes is private, nonpolitical and nondenominational. It is bypassing tradition to pioneer in new patterns of educational organization and standards.

Adlai Stevenson and I were guided around the campus by Jaime Samper, rector and administrative head of the university, and by Ramón de Zubiria, the assistant rector. (Lleras Camargo, president of Colombia, was the former rector.) The buildings are modest and inexpensively constructed—one is a former jail. We were told that there are currently about 800 students, of whom 300 are women. But there are no students on the university council, and the students are given no legal rights of any kind over the operation of the university. Samper tells them that every student has the full right at all times to be heard, but that no student has any right beyond this—except to apply himself to his own development. There have been no student strikes except one for one day. (The premedical students stayed away from classes in a protest against low entrance requirements at the national medical school; they wanted other entrants to be as well prepared as they were.) De Zubiria told us, "At other Colombian universities, the students have representation on the board of trustees, but not here. We handle the students differently. We are in permanent dialogue with them!"

De Zubiria described students in most Latin-American universities as "passive" in the classroom. The professors "lecture at them." At the University of the Andes the students are urged to be "active." In the classrooms that we visited, the groups were small and the students were participating in discussions. One interesting room we visited was a "laboratory" in which a large group of students were studying English. (Unlike some Latin-American universities which teach French as a second language, the University of the Andes teaches English.) Each student sat in a little cubicle with earphones on his head. On the screen at the end of the room was a still picture in color. The teachers were in the control room at the back. We put on the teacher's earphones and heard, on prerecorded tape, an instructor say in English, "The furniture in the room is yellow"—as was shown in the picture on the screen—and then the entire group would immediately repeat the sentence. The teacher could tune in on any student she wished. I said to Governor Stevenson, "These students are pronouncing more English in this one hour of instruction than you and I had a chance to pronounce French in a full term of instruction when we were boys."

One part of the university's program in which Samper and de Zubiria take special pride is its affiliation with universities in the United States. After two years of pre-engineering training at the University of the Andes, the brightest boys are selected to spend their next two years in the United States. Their families are approached to see how much of the cost they can carry, and the balance is loaned to the students from a university fund which now totals 2,000,000 pesos.

De Zubiria told us that several European governments have approached the university, wanting their universities to participate in the program, but that he prefers the United States. He feels the atmosphere in the United States is "best for the boys," that they go from a "tense environment" in Colombia to find tolerance in the United States. They find freedom of discussion among political parties, freedom of religion and, most importantly of all, they learn the "dignity of work." They find themselves rooming with boys who, "though they may be Nelson Rockefeller's sons," may be working in cafeterias or filling stations. Thus these young Colombian engineers "come back to

Colombia and aren't afraid to work; we are proud of the fact that they come back knowing how to put grease on their hands; we like the United States because it exposes them to this new culture."

Samper explained to us—somewhat apologetically and just as any university administrator in the U.S. might—that one of the big problems of the university is money. "A year's study abroad for one student," he said, "represents an investment of up to 25,000 pesos and that, no matter how you look at it, is a great deal of money." And of course the money is most difficult to raise because, as I have pointed out, the giving of large sums for endowments and trusts for educational purposes is almost unknown in Latin America.

I left the University of the Andes with the conviction that this small, struggling institution is a most important venture, with the prospect of a remarkable future. What this one university is seeking to do can conceivably set a pattern for the rest of Colombia and indeed for all of Latin America.

I do not mean to suggest that the University of the Andes is the only well-administered Latin-American university. Among the institutions I happened to visit this one seemed to me to have the best potential for creating a new pattern. I have been assured, for example, that another new Colombian university, the 15-year-old Universidad del Valle at Cali, in the rich Cauca valley, is also outstanding—indeed, that it is "the future medical center of Latin America." It is already staffed with 65 full-time professors and has a salary level high enough to hold the best men, thanks to strong budget support from the provinciai government and to grants for medicine from the Rockefeller foundation. Still another beacon of progress is the University of Concepción in Chile, which, like the University of the Andes, is relatively new. Though it receives some government support, it regards itself as private. It has a campus including dormitories and its vigorous new rector, David Stitchkin, has adopted the U.S. departmental system in creating institutes of physics, chemistry, biology and mathematics. Delegates to a UNESCO meeting in Paris in 1958 declared Stitchkin's "Concepción reform plan" to be UNESCO's "pilot project for university organization" in Latin America. Still another institution of special interest is the Institute of Technology and Higher Education of Monterrey, Mexico, sometimes called the "M.I.T. of Latin America," which is a completely U.S.-type institution.

I am persuaded that it is greatly in the interest of U.S. policy to assist universities of such types as the University of the Andes—that is, with a nonpolitical governing board and a rector appointed by the board, with deans and teachers appointed by the board on the recommendation of the rector. Such universities, with more backing, could quickly exercise a powerful influence over the whole course of higher education in Latin America.

I should perhaps conclude this section by applauding the liberal motivation and the drive for autonomy of the universities of Latin America. But let these seek also the sustenance of real education. Only thus can they breed in their students clear thinking, honest judgment and lucid habits of mind. Only thus can liberalism combat the dragon's teeth being planted by Communists who have for decades been concentrating on the Latin-American universities. Víctor Andrés Belaunde of Peru recently charged publicly that Latin-American students, through their accent on political activity, are learning to think and work only for the purpose of obtaining power. They are not learning to build. Even worse, he said, they are not receiving in their institutions of higher learning the necessary intellectual and moral discipline to enable them to judge how to build well. Here is the front line in the long-range conflict now raging in Latin America.

I shall have some recommendations to make about U.S. policy toward Latin-American education in the concluding chapters. As with the problem of economic development, and the problem of keeping communism under control, the Latin-American nations themselves must and will be responsible for the education of their own people. The friendliest neighbor can only help as it can—and the direct help it can give is likely to be less at the lower educational levels. Raúl Prebisch confessed to me, "The very extensive illiteracy in Latin America is something for which we are ourselves exclusively responsible."

Nevertheless, the most intelligent and farsighted way in which a good neighbor can help the Latin-American countries to stand on their own feet is to help them help themselves in those areas in which help is welcome and most easily given. A central and pivotal area under this neighborly goal is to help them educate and train tomorrow's leaders. This program should immediately be greatly accelerated.

5

How Can the United States Best Help Latin America Help Itself?

Alfredo Vítolo, Argentina's hard-driving Minister of the Interior, told us that the problem of the United States with Latin Americans is "to regain our confidence." Pres. Franklin D. Roosevelt, he said, had won the psychological and spiritual confidence of the Latin-American people. "When he came here, he was hailed as a world leader." The minister added that visits such as we were making could have "tremendous repercussions, because they are objective." He gave it as his opinion that "the human element" is even more important to Latin America than financial aid. Governor Stevenson later stressed this observation. I agree that it has higher importance than most bankers or economists concede. Along with financial and technical aid, the Latin Americans want sympathetic understanding from their powerful neighbor to the north. They think they want the renewal of an attitude that they feel has been warped in recent years.

One influential and experienced foreign minister put a part of the problem this way: "I hope the United States will listen more.

Won't you listen to advice from South America? Whether it's good advice or whether it's bad, whether you follow it or whether you don't—won't you listen?"

But "listening" is only the beginning. What do we do about what we hear? And indeed, what do the Latin leaders themselves do? One of the most influential members of the U.S. Senate, Mike Mansfield of Montana, has described what we and they shall learn when we listen: "The social structures of many nations of the region are seriously out of date and cannot endure in their present form in the second half of the twentieth century. They cannot endure for the simple reason that they do not deliver enough education, enough food, shelter and clothing, enough medical aid, enough of the conveniences that are taken for granted in this country and are relatively commonplace in Western Europe and even in Soviet Russia. Most important, they do not provide for a sufficient number of people that intangible but essential element of prideful participation in the present and hope for the future which is the keynote of political stability."

Here is the problem, and most brilliantly summarized not only for us but for the Latin leaders who seek to play a dynamic and constructive role in the social and political development of the future.

U.S. Policies of the Past

To a historian who looks back over the decades to the beginning of our relationship with the Latin-American countries it is obvious that the United States has a heritage of genuine friendship—as well as a heritage of unhappy blunders and misunderstandings. We gave early recognition to the new Latin-American states as they struggled for and finally won their independence in the years 1810–1824. Still a young nation ourselves, we applauded and encouraged the colonies of Latin America to free themselves from Spain, Portugal and France.

On August 27, 1810, Pres. James Madison's secretary of state issued instructions to Joel R. Poinsett, his representative who was about to leave on a tour of South America: "Diffuse the impression that the United States cherish the sincerest good will toward the people of Spanish America as neighbors, as belonging to the same portion of the globe, and as having a mutual interest in cultivating friendly intercourse." The secretary added, in view of the revolutionary activities of Simón Bolívar and others: "In the event of a political separation from the parent country, and of the establishment of an independent system of National Government, it will coincide with the sentiments and policy of the United States to promote the most friendly relations and the most liberal intercourse between the inhabitants of this Hemisphere, as having all a common interest, and as lying under a common obligation to maintain that system of peace, justice and good will which is the only source of happiness for nations." Indeed, this instruction can be termed the origin of the "good neighbor policy." (And perhaps I should add that Poinsett brought back from Mexico a beautiful and neighborly flower which not unnaturally became known as the poinsettia.)

THE MONROE DOCTRINE, set forth on December 2, 1823, by Pres. James Monroe as part of a message to congress, said this: "We owe it, therefore, to candor, and to the amicable relations existing between the United States and those (European) powers, to declare that we should consider any attempt on their part to extend their system to any portion of this hemisphere as dangerous to our peace and safety." Little importance was attached to this statement of U.S. policy at the time; and indeed the doctrine was violated by the French in Mexico during the Civil War. Many scholars have contended it would have had but little strategic meaning without the undeclared support of Britain and its navy. British world policy throughout the 19th century was geared to maintaining a balance of power in Europe, and Latin America was an element in this balance.

It was not until the (Theodore) Roosevelt corollary in 1904 that the Monroe Doctrine aroused resentment in Latin America. President Roosevelt said that "in the Western Hemisphere the adherence of the United States to the Monroe Doctrine may force the United States, however reluctantly, in flagrant cases of such wrongdoing or impotence, to the exercise of an international police power." His thesis was that the doctrine not only forbade intervention from Europe in Latin America but actually sanctioned intervention by the United States in order to eliminate the risk of such intervention by others.

This has been called the policy of the "big stick," and the Latin-American countries remember it well. The "big stick" was carried, and we were not speaking softly, in our first intervention in Santo Domingo (now the Dominican Republic); in our acquisition of the Panama canal; in our five Caribbean interventions; and later in interventions extending through that in Mexico during World War I; indeed, U.S. troops were not entirely withdrawn from certain island republics until the time of Franklin D. Roosevelt. In every such instance U.S. purpose was allegedly twofold—to restore order where a state of anarchy and chaos threatened, and to protect the basic security of the United States. Except in the case of the Panama canal, there was no intent on the part of the United States to annex or exploit (although there was of course the property of Americans to consider). In 1908 Secretary of State Elihu Root summed up United States Cuban policy: "We don't want Cuba to ourselves; we cannot permit any other power to get possession of her and, to prevent the necessity of one and the possibility of the other, we want her to govern herself decently and in order." More than 50 years later these same words could be used to describe our present considerations and the qualms which spring from them over the government of Fidel Castro.

THE GOOD NEIGHBOR POLICY.—The fears produced in Latin America by Theodore Roosevelt's "big stick" were not begun to be allayed until March 4, 1933, when Franklin D. Roosevelt in his inaugural address proclaimed his so-called good neighbor policy. He said: "I would dedicate this nation to the policy of the good neighbor—the neighbor who resolutely respects himself and, because he does so, respects the rights of others—the neighbor who respects his obligations and respects the sanctity of agreements in and with a world of neighbors."

Some historians argue that the political implementation of the good neighbor policy—for example the United States' unilateral backing off from the Platt Amendment, which as part of Cuba's constitution gave the U.S. the right to intervene if necessary in Cuban affairs—was too precipitate. They believe such hasty and unplanned withdrawal opened the way for such dictatatorial regimes as in the Dominican Republic, Nicaragua and Cuba.

However, Latin-American leaders today speak with unanimity and enthusiasm of Roosevelt and his policy. The good neighbor policy was not a concrete dollars-and-cents operation such as the Marshall plan in Europe, which provided specific dollars for specific purposes. It was largely an attitude. It generated a state of mind. As one Latin-American leader put it to me, "You thought of us then as a trusted and worthwhile friend. That," he insisted, "is the essential point of difference between then and now."

Thus during the 1930's we gave the Latin-American countries a feeling that we were *simpático*. Today they still feel that we then treated them as partners in the Americas, that we then accorded them the dignity of equals, that we listened, that we carefully avoided positioning them as "beggars at the table of the rich man." Nelson Rockefeller's appointment by President Roosevelt as Co-ordinator of Inter-American Affairs helped to symbolize the good neighbor attitude of the immediate prewar period. Rockefeller, as an inheritor of the Roosevelt tradition and as a great North American entrepreneur in Latin America who has mastered their language, is today a giant figure throughout the continent. He is the citizen of the United States second in stature only to Adlai Stevenson, who has seemed in Latin eyes to be F.D.R.'s lineal descendant.

Further Latin Criticisms of Recent U.S. Policy

In Santiago, Chile, Governor Stevenson and I invited letters from students and scholars after an all-morning meeting with them. This meeting had been precipitated by a letter of protest from the students to President Eisenhower on his visit to Santiago, shortly before our own arrival. The Federation of Chilean Students, a non-Communist group (their letter invoked the name of the Holy Spirit), had addressed to him a long and eloquent communication which was widely discussed throughout Latin America and which recited many of the grievances I have outlined in early sections. The letter spoke of the "merciless exploitation" of Latin America by European and North American capital, and of the need for "just prices" for Latin-American commodities. It argued that the U.S. had failed to provide initiative for a nonmilitary system of security in the hemisphere; that we had supported dictators; that we had not encouraged the economic integration of Latin America or "collaborated decisively" in Latin America's industrialization. It contended that because 40% (*sic*) of Latin America's population is illiterate and because two thirds are in a "chronic state of malnutrition," "the politics of the *status quo*" are inadequate.

One of the letters that came as a follow-up to Governor Stevenson and me, which summarized the theme of many others, captured much of the present critical feeling toward the United States. It was written in English, a compliment to us. It is too long to print in full but this condensed version makes the characteristic points:

> Dear Mr. Senator:
> Dear Mr. Stevenson:
> You are arriving at our land mainly to acquire deeper knowledge about Latin America and make a personal inquiry about the way we feel about United States policy. It would not be fair to leave you dependent only on the too conventional official people, for national pride would never allow them to speak freely all of the truths which I am going to tell you as if you were old friends.
>
> You have surely been told about the hearty reception given to President Eisenhower, which demonstrated first of all the tremendously charming personality of IKE, and besides that we

Chileans really like the USA. But still you must know that there is a hidden sore and even hard feelings in some of us for the States.

We admire and feel pride in the immense role played by our American friend in maintaining by himself half of the whole world; the USSR is doing likewise to the other half. But even when we know perfectly well that the USA has no obligation to help us or anybody else, nevertheless under the circumstances the proportion of the help received by us is shameful: the loans and gifts to Europe, including the enemies, during the Marshall Plan were annually over 5,000 million dollars—while for all Latin America it was only a matter of a few hundred! What we felt, you can put in your far-western way. Imagine a cowboy who enters a cantina and shouts loudly: "Wine for everybody, except this fellow—for whom a glass of water will do!"

The poor fellow is we Latin Americans. Of course the cowboy was under no obligation to treat anybody, but under the circumstances . . . ! So we felt that it was we who really lost the war—because even your enemies received better treatment.

Unfortunately there has been a big gap between the words and deeds of American leaders. For instance, Mr. Eisenhower said in his historic address at Columbia University, The Chance for Peace: "Instead of atomic bombs humanity needs more food to combat the oldest enemy of mankind—HUNGER."

These were undoubtedly beautiful words, but a few days later some Latin American countries were granted a loan in armaments to fulfill the duties imposed by the Treaty of Continental Defense. . . .

In the meantime the two colossi of our time, Ike and Khrushchev, are preparing to meet each other to determine the fate of mankind. Both are equally powerful and likewise of tremendous charming personality; meanwhile we ordinary people can only pray: May God enlighten them and allow them to bring peace to this world in such dreadful fear!!

Well, Mr. Stevenson and Mr. Senator, my intentions are well-meant, so I can only apologize for my rough sincerity. These were pretty difficult nasty things to say to noble guests like you, but you seek truth, not to be flattered. I gave *our truth.* If I am mistaken we are all to be blamed on account of misinformation. But somebody has to say it once, and somebody else has to listen to it.

Sincerely yours,
Augustín Arriagada

Merced 314, Santiago de Chile, 5 March 1960

Agustín Arriagada's central criticism, that the United States is oriented too much to Europe and Asia and too little to Latin America, was frequently voiced. Diógenes Taboada, Argentina's Foreign Minister, told us that most Latin Americans feel this way. But he gladly conceded that, in his own judgment, without the Marshall Plan Europe would have been lost to Communism. (Governor Stevenson commented that he wished more people in Latin America knew this!)

A second criticism in the letter is that United States leaders say one thing and do another—that our deeds do not live up to our words. This also was charged against the U.S. in various ways throughout our trip.

Some misconceptions in this letter are instructive: the low figure on U.S. financial support of Latin America and the implied belief that many loans are only in the form of armaments. Arriagada is correct, however, that our Latin loans and grants are a relatively small proportion of our world-wide total. There was no Latin-American equivalent to the Marshall Plan, through which the U.S. helped rebuild economies in Europe that had been ruptured by the war. Nor has there been fully equivalent aid to Latin America since the Marshall Plan. For the years 1956–60, the U.S. Government extended economic aid to underdeveloped countries totalling $11,494,000,000. Of this total, only $1,419,000,000—or 12%—went to the American Republics.

Unhappy also is the misconception that the United States and the Soviet Union are engaged in splitting the world between them—and seemingly with little difference in their power attitudes!

There are two dominant and incontrovertible facts which cut through the emotional attitudes and political propaganda which becloud the relationships between the United States and the Latin-American countries. The first is implicit in the traditional phrase Latin Americans apply to us—the colossus of the north. Yes, the United States is powerful and wealthy. Yes, Latin America is relatively weak and poor. Yes, Latin America needs our help desperately.

The second dominant fact is that we need the Latin Americans. Perhaps over the long pull we need them as much as they need us. We need their resources. We need their friendship. In all probability we need them if we are to survive as a free nation. They are thus one of the keys to our future.

What, then, should our policies be toward Latin America? At the federal level, how should we seek to implement our policies in terms of appropriations and legislative acts? Over and above this, what might we do as U.S. communities, as trustees of foundations and universities, as scholars and businessmen, as philanthropists and as individual citizens? I do not pretend to have all, or even most of the answers, or any formula, either psychological or political or financial or a combination of all three. The relationships that the 20 individual republics of Latin America have with each other and with the United States are far too complex to permit a "packaged" solution or indeed any permanent solution. Further, the problem is complicated by the pride of the Latins. Often our help will be effective only when it is disguised. It can never be gratuitous—or forced. We can help only on their terms as well as ours—in their way as well as our own.

In my suggestions which follow I have not attempted to present the costs to the United States of any given idea, much less the total cost. Some of the best ideas, however, are not costly—while some of the ideas being advocated widely today, which are least effective, may prove very costly indeed. I break my suggestions down into four broad categories: ideas primarily in the political field; those in the general area of economic policy; those dealing with higher education; and finally ideas which I classify broadly as cultural and informational. The alternative to clear-cut and constructive policies in these areas is not pleasant to contemplate. Eduardo Santos, former President of Colombia and world-renowned publisher of *El Tiempo* of Bogota, poses it harshly: "As things are now going," he said, "the greatest upheaval in history is brewing in Latin America. In 5, 10 or 15 years, unless the United States acts, you'll see country after country explode. The Cuban upheaval will seem mild in comparison." Perhaps Santos is wrong but, as I hope this book demonstrates, it is the part of wisdom in the formulation of U.S. policy to assume that he may be right.

Suggestions in the Area of Politics

We must begin with political ideas. These are more difficult, less easy to pursue with confidence and even more hazardous than economic proposals. We can, however, develop many specific and concrete ideas, within the framework of the viewpoint expressed in this article, if we seek them aggressively and pursue them boldly. Not all will succeed and we must reconcile ourselves to occasional failures. I submit the following few political ideas as tentative. One of my major objectives is to stimulate discussion. These are mere samples—and any student of the hemisphere could list many others. The point is that we of the U.S. should seek fresh and dynamic new political approaches—open our minds to them and then be prepared to implement them in terms of political leadership and legislative action within our own country.

First and foremost, we must do what we can honestly to consult much more with the Latin-American governments. We must give far more than lip service to the idea of a partnership of the Americas. Often our actions are questioned not so much because of what we do as because of how we do it. The Latins are acutely conscious of their weaknesses. They don't want us to remind them of them constantly. Because they are relatively weak, it is the more important that they know what is going on—and that we expose ourselves to their views about what is going on. They need not be—and are not—weak in the vital area of ideas.

Rural schoolhouse in Peru. Senator Benton describes the task of providing an adequate public-school system in Latin America as "monumental."

Credit: Cornell Capa—Magnum Photos

TOWARD DISARMAMENT.—Perhaps the best quick example of a big political idea is disarmament. In every country we visited we asked top officials, "Why doesn't Latin America take world leadership in disarmament?" The United States now assumes re-

Credit: John Fell Stevenson

Luncheon with former President Kubitschek of Brazil. "Governor Stevenson and I were impressed by the personality and ability of most of the political leaders . . ."

sponsibility for defense of the hemisphere, and the Organization of American States takes responsibility for defense against aggression within the hemisphere. Yet some countries spend as much as 50% of their national budgets on armaments. Mexico has the best record with only about 7%. (We were laughingly assured by an official in Chile that this was because of the two countries which border Mexico: the country on its north—the United States—is much too big to attack, and the country on the south—Guatemala—is too small to worry about!)

I believe a disarmament proposal may be the most important single political objective in Latin America which the United States can now promote. I believe also that such a proposal could focus Latin-American moral strength on a critical point of world politics. President Alessandri of Chile is taking leadership in an effort to advance this cause.

Although prestige is surely a major factor in armaments, many Latins blame the unnecessary military expenditures of the past on border disputes, particularly those of Chile and Argentina and of Ecuador and Peru. President López Mateos of Mexico told Governor Stevenson and me that the Ecuador-Peru boundary problem must be cleared up before any general disarmament agreement could be worked out. A week later in Bogotá, Colombia's President Lleras Camargo expressed the same conviction.

In 1941 this dispute led to a pitched war between Peru and Ecuador, with thousands killed. Now under an uneasy truce, Peru, a country so poor that its per capita annual income is only about $100, is said to pour as much as 50% of its entire national budget into military expenditures. (Peru refuses to trade with Ecuador; it boycotts Ecuadorian products.)

Ecuador retaliated to a recent purchase by Peru of obsolete cruisers from Great Britain by purchasing jet planes, even though the jets are "practically out of the country before they take off" as the president of one country put it. So intense is the feeling in Ecuador that toward the close of 1960 there were reports that Ecuador might turn to Cuba for help. Chile, which has had its own border troubles in the past with Peru, and whose army occupied Lima in 1881, finds it difficult to hold down its military expenditures. Argentina, in turn, with an approximate 2,700-mi. common border with Chile and a long-standing quarrel over the ownership of a group of desolate islands in the Straits of Magellan, adds an aircraft carrier to its navy. Brazil doesn't want to lag behind. This is the so-called "chain reaction." It is heartening that, as I write this, Argentina and Chile have agreed to submit their dispute to arbitration.

When we reached Ecuador and Peru the problem of course was made to look highly complex. "The disputed area has been Peruvian for 50 years," former Foreign Minister Javier Correa Elias told us at a meeting of Peruvian political and intellectual leaders called in part to demonstrate Peru's unanimity on the boundary dispute. This was at the height of an Ecuadorian presidential campaign. We were told, "Peru not only has the Rio Treaty behind its rights, but has historical background and precedents as well. What is Peru supposed to do if every time there is an election in Ecuador the problem is tossed at us once more by Ecuadorian politicians?"

Governor Stevenson spoke up sharply to say that the settlement of the border dispute should be reached promptly. He pointed out that it is extremely difficult for the United States to justify to its taxpayers its financial help to Ecuador and Peru when such large percentages of their budgets are spent on armaments.

In Ecuador we discussed this subject at length with Galo Plaza. The handsome 54-year-old former President, with a lifetime of distinguished public service behind him, was then the Liberal candidate (unsuccessful) for the presidency in the June 1960 elections.

"We should have an arms limitation conference as soon as possible," the former president told us. "Such a conference for all of South America may help force Ecuador and Peru to settle our own problems. I regret Ecuador's present expenditures on arms, but what can we do? Peru is spending far more."

Plaza told us that better economic relationships between the two countries would help. "It would be far cheaper for Peru to import agricultural products from Ecuador, bringing them down the coast, than it is for her to boycott us and to import over the Andes from Brazil. There is a complementary economy in our two countries, and an improvement in our trade relations would help settle our boundary dispute."

Of course Latin-American countries do not pile up armaments solely because they fear each other. National pride, the ambition of military cliques, internal as well as external political pressures—all contribute to the military build-up. The tragedy is that while there is not one country that we visited that could not productively use its entire military budget for the training of teachers and the building of schools—leadership has thus far been lacking in the hemisphere to help shift the money for guns into textbooks. The U.S. can indeed play a much more vital role in helping to stimulate such leadership.

RELOCATION OF OAS HEADQUARTERS.—Why should the United States itself not raise the question of whether the headquarters of the Organization of American States ought to be moved from Washington to a location in Latin America—perhaps to Panamá? I heard much criticism of the OAS on the ground that it is a captive agency of the United States, and that its policies are directed to suit United States interests rather than the interests of the Latin-American countries. By physically separating the OAS from the United States we would perhaps remove an important psychological block. I favor proposing such a shift for consideration even if the ambassadors to the OAS decide that they prefer Washington to Panama City or anywhere else—as they well may do. I like putting the responsibility upon them for review of this question. Let them take it off our shoulders where many seek to put it.

We should give consideration to a plan for internationalizing the Canal Zone, perhaps under control of the Organization of American States, even though both the administration in Washington and the government of Panamá have been on record as opposing such a step. When Theodore Roosevelt negotiated the independence of Panamá from Colombia in 1903 he created a country with a built-in scar. This scar, the ten-mile-wide Canal Zone that bisects Panamá, rankles in the hearts of Panamanians and provides tinder for their political wars. The situation has not been helped by the attitude of the U.S. inhabitants of the Canal Zone, many of whom seldom if ever leave the zone.

The canal's importance is largely economic today, rather than military. Its hemispheric internationalization might provide important ideological dividends. It could not only provide a home for OAS, if the OAS wanted it as a home; it could help support the OAS and its projects.

ATTITUDE TOWARD DICTATORS.—On the psychological front, the United States needs to find some dramatic way of showing that we really do not like dictators. True, we seek to avoid intervention in the domestic politics of any foreign nation. True, we have felt that we must deal with dictators "correctly" when they come to power. But we do not have to show them special favors. Governor Stevenson and I were constantly reminded that the United States has the reputation of approving of right-wing dictators in the hemisphere as long as they confine their activities to their own countries and do not bother the United States. Over and over we were reminded of the honorific medals we of the U.S. have unhappily bestowed. These medallic symbols, such as the order of merit bestowed on Venezuela's dictator Pérez Jiménez in 1954 by John Foster Dulles, the medal to Odría, the Peruvian dictator the same year, and to General Francisco Tabernilla, the chief of Batista's air force in 1957, offset hundreds of millions of dollars in U.S. good deeds. If it were legally legitimate for us to kick Pérez Jiménez out of the United States today, I suspect this one act would do us more political good in Latin America than another $250,000,000 in capital for the Inter-American bank. At the very least, we should make it crystal clear that we don't like having Pérez Jiménez in political asylum here, that we do not approve of dictators of the political right any more than we do of the left, that the people of the U.S. regret Batista and will welcome developments in their countries which will lead to the reform of the Trujillo regime, to the fall of the Somoza brothers of Nicaragua, of Alfred Stroessner of Paraguay or of any future dictator.

FOREIGN SERVICE STANDARDS.—We should set a higher standard in our appointment of ambassadors and continue energetically to build up the caliber of all of our overseas personnel. Top men are available. They should be aggressively sought and intensively instructed. They should be well paid—and adequately underwritten with expense allowances. We should bring them together frequently into regional meetings so that they can have the first-hand benefit of each other's experiences. There is a major chance to improve communications among our embassies in the Latin-American countries. Many of the problems they face are common problems. They do not have sufficient opportunity to exchange views. They are too isolated from each other, just like the countries to which they are assigned.

Fluency in the language, respect for local culture, ability and willingness to meet Latin Americans on any cultural plane—these must become marks of the representatives of the United States. One of my acquaintances in Peru told me that in 1959, when a distinguished group of Peruvians, including the foreign minister, met to observe the centennial of the death of the great U.S. historian W. H. Prescott, author of *The Conquest of Peru*, no representative of our ambassador and no prominent U.S. resident appeared at the ceremony. This is not typical. Our representatives work hard and constantly at this kind of ceremonial. I cite it merely to show that we are constantly watched and that, no matter how well we do on the big things, there are also the little things on which we are also under scrutiny.

In the Area of Economic Policy

Here above all, here and in the field of education, the problem is how to help the Latin-American countries help themselves. The problem is far more complex than mere money. We cannot do the job with bigger and bigger appropriations, nor can we buy good will merely with dollars. Indeed, our generosity in some quarters will only generate demands for more and more. Many an individual and country has sorrowfully learned that it is very difficult to give away money and thereby earn gratitude. Thus our loans and grants must be handled with discrimination and great care. And monies spent on the economic front must be supplemented by substantial sums for cultural and educational activities such as scholarships or exchanges of professors and others on an accelerating scale.

On the encouraging side is the fact that Governor Stevenson and I were impressed with the intelligent approach of many of Latin America's leaders to the economic problems of their countries.

Prebisch, perhaps the most widely known Latin-American economic theorist and whose views I have approvingly cited earlier, of course has his critics. Among these, in the United States, are the authors of a report for the Committee for Economic Development, of which I was the founding vice-chairman during the war. This report prepared for this most liberal of U.S. business groups, looking toward a major study of economic growth in Latin America, went so far as to ask itself whether "Prebischism" may not be "the major obstacle to Latin America's development." The report suggests that Prebisch places entirely too much weight on the public sector of the economy. (In Prebisch's own Argentina public enterprise is now in eclipse; for example, as the railroads steadily lose money, many Argentinians rue the $600,000,000 Perón spent to buy them from the British who first developed them. President Frondizi recently invited private oil companies to develop Argentina's petroleum resources—though only at the risk of inviting political attacks for permitting foreign exploitation.)

In my judgment, Prebisch is misunderstood in the report to the CED and so too may be the needs of the Latin-American economy. In a memorandum Prebisch sent Governor Stevenson and me, outlining his views, he wrote:

> I have a deep belief in the enormous potentialities of private initiative in Latin America, but I am equally persuaded that, as presently functioning, it cannot, by itself, generate the rate of economic development necessary to satisfy the rising needs of our fast growing population nor effectively respond to the challenge of the Soviet method of economic development. . . .
>
> I have arrived at the seemingly paradoxical conclusion that in order to strengthen the dynamic vitality of the system of private

> initiative in this part of the world it is indispensable that the state should have a clear and far-sighted determination to influence and channel economic forces through a deliberate process of economic planning.

In talking economic development with Prebisch, Governor Stevenson remarked, "I am one American who is not afraid of the word 'planning'!" I concur; I happen to be a lifelong practitioner of "free enterprise." I have developed four businesses of my own, and I have faith in the dynamism of a market economy. But I sympathize with the Latin-American leaders who complained to me that their critics from the U.S. become more doctrinaire about market economics the farther they get from home. Many such critics refuse to recognize that the United States itself has a mixed economy. We of the U.S. have our own forms of federal government action in road building, power development, flood and harbor control, housing, finance and countless other fields.

I agree with Prebisch that government planning is indispensable if Latin America is to make the most effective use of its resources or even to achieve a climate which can best foster private enterprise. Decisions at the governmental level must be made, for example, on how important education is to economic development, and what financial priority it should get; on tax and budget policies as they affect economic development; on the degree of regulation and control of utilities; on policies affecting the growth of cities and the spread of slums. As the rural population crowds into the cities, training facilities need to be established. There will be a rise of many new occupations and an expansion of many service fields. Technical assistance on how to plan for this extension can be of great help.

Thus the United States should not hesitate to help its neighbors to plan. Without government planning, there can be only limited opportunity for free or private enterprise. Innumerable avenues are open to us, not least of which is the United Nations.

ELIMINATION OF ARTIFICIAL TRADE BARRIERS.—Further, we should try more sympathetically to help the Latin-American countries get together with each other. For the past several years I have been serving on the so-called U.S. Committee for a United Europe, a group that has had the blessing of the state department and the administration. We should long since have established a U.S. Committee for a United Latin America. Such a committee's first goal should have been to help Latin America build a common market by eliminating or reducing barriers to trade between and among the 20 republics. The criticism that the United States has dragged its feet on the subject of a common market in Latin America is justified; our failure to help provide leadership has deterred these countries from progress toward unification. Foreign Minister Diógenes Taboada of Argentina told us that some of the seven countries who recently signed the common market agreement on which I have reported earlier "don't yet know what it's all about." The United States should—even though belatedly—help them find out, and should help them work toward implementing and expanding this hesitant step toward a common market for all of Latin America—and indeed I would hope, for the entire western hemisphere. We should proceed towards a policy that will eliminate trade barriers between the United States and Latin America as rapidly as possible (though I concede that this may involve some U.S. government help in the readjustment of our own domestic industry). I am wholly opposed to our excise tax on South American copper, for example. It should be repealed. We should not provide incentives to exhaust our own remaining copper reserves. Further, I am opposed to U.S. restrictive legislation against the importation of lead, zinc or any other commodity.

We of the United States must not look upon a program of reducing barriers merely as a neighborly opportunity to "do good." It is an opportunity to help these countries develop their own economies to the point where they will be self-sustaining and thereby cease to be a drain on us and become a vastly increased market for U.S. goods. We should not permanently protect our domestic producers against Latin-American competition at the

Table V.—Latin-American Republics' Trade with the U.S. in U.S. $ (1959)

Country	*Total exports*	*To U.S.*	*Total imports*	*From U.S.*
Argentina	1,009,000,000	124,489,000	993,000,000	229,802,000
Bolivia	59,600,000	6,905,000	65,000,000	23,313,000
Brazil	1,282,000,000	611,172,000	1,374,000,000	401,388,000
Chile	497,000,000	156,133,000	413,000,000	136,432,000
Colombia	467,000,000	339,794,000	408,000,000	204,161,000
Costa Rica	80,000,000	32,709,000	103,000,000	40,762,000
Cuba	635,000,000	467,219,000	610,000,000	434,747,000
Dominican Republic .	130,000,000	75,151,000	117,538,000	59,482,000
Ecuador	140,000,000	60,181,000	95,000,000	48,503,000
El Salvador	113,000,000	37,377,000	100,000,000	36,843,000
Guatemala	118,000,000	64,906,000	132,000,000	64,084,000
Haiti	28,000,000	16,075,000	30,000,000	23,410,000
Honduras	70,000,000	24,588,000	62,000,000	32,335,000
Mexico	756,000,000	428,649,000	1,007,000,000	726,434,000
Nicaragua	65,000,000	15,396,000	66,800,000	27,585,000
Panamá	34,000,000	24,938,000	97,000,000	90,066,000
Paraguay	31,196,000	8,457,000	26,194,000	7,814,000
Peru	311,000,000	105,340,000	294,000,000	121,590,000
Uruguay	98,000,000	19,006,000	160,000,000	33,338,000
Venezuela	2,369,493,000	881,066,000	1,408,025,000	734,735,000

expense of the U.S. as a whole. Experience demonstrates that by far the best foreign markets for U.S. goods are those regions with well-developed and industrialized economies of their own.

Government Incentives to Investment.—To encourage more initiative by U.S. private business in Latin America we should re-examine all of our laws affecting incentives for overseas investments, including our tax laws. In an important address to the senate in February 1960 Sen. George Smathers of Florida said: "U.S. investors complain—and I think rightly—that our federal tax laws operate to deprive them of the advantages of tax concessions granted by other governments in an effort to attract capital." And when Undersecretary of State, C. Douglas Dillon "invited" other countries to discuss with the U.S. the development of treaties under which the U.S. would give assurance that a lowering of local taxes on earnings of U.S. companies operating abroad would not merely have the effect of increasing their U.S. taxes.[1]

Tax incentives are not the only means available to stimulate foreign private investment. We need a great extension of our present guarantee program, providing insurance against non-

[1] The U.S. income tax vitally affects private investment in Latin America. Until June 1961, the only important tax incentive given to U.S. corporations investing abroad was the device of the "western hemisphere trade corporation." The rate of U.S. corporate tax applied to qualifying corporations was 14% less than the regular United States rate; thus the maximum rate was 38% instead of 52%. However, to qualify as a western hemisphere trade corporation the company had to derive 95% or more of its gross income from sources outside the United States. Because of the 95% requirement, in practice this device has offered incentives principally to companies engaged in the extractive industries or export operations. And recent rulings of the U.S. treasury have made its usefulness as an incentive for export operations increasingly doubtful.

For a number of years Rep. Thomas Hale Boggs of Louisiana had proposed extending the status of the western hemisphere trade corporations to all domestic corporations which derive their income from active conduct of trade or business anywhere abroad, not only in western hemisphere countries. The Boggs bill also made it easier to qualify as a western hemisphere trade corporation by providing that only 90%—not 95%—of income be derived from sources outside of the United States. Boggs received little support for his bill until 1960 when a bipartisan majority of both houses of congress acted favorably on this part of his recommendations.

An even more important proposal of Representative Boggs would be to permit domestic corporations, qualifying as foreign business corporations, to defer payment of U.S. taxes on income accumulated abroad, provided such income is reinvested abroad. At present, only foreign subsidiaries which are not branches of a U.S. corporation, but corporate entities organized under the laws of a foreign country, are able by deferral of the U.S. tax to reinvest the greater portion of their foreign earnings. But foreign incorporation requires expatriation of capital. For this and other reasons, important segments of the U.S. business community have been unwilling to follow this route. It is to be hoped that the 87th congress will approve this latest important proposal of Representative Boggs.

Aside from the question of incentives, adequate relief from international double taxation is necessary if foreign investments are to be increased. At present, United States corporations are taxed on all income earned abroad by branches of these corporations in foreign countries. (Again, foreign subsidiaries are not taxed by the U.S. except on income actually returned to the parent company.) Although the U.S. will grant credits—against the U.S. tax imposed on the same income—for payments of foreign income and excess

commercial risks which have inhibited U.S. companies from doing business abroad. Such risks are those of expropriation which have recently wiped out hundreds of millions of dollars of U.S. private investments in Cuba. The Export-Import bank announced during March 1960 a new policy under which its export guarantee program, which had become all but moribund, would be stepped up.

We were told by U.S. businessmen in many areas of Latin America that they are being undersold by the Italians, French, West Germans, Swiss, Canadians, Japanese and others, partly because exporters of these countries can offer better credit terms. The West German government has been the most liberal in underwriting its exporters. Indeed, European countries have felt it necessary to set up the so-called Berne union under which they seek to control excesses in state guarantees of export credits. The limit of such guarantees now agreed upon is six years and the top credit is usually 80% of selling price. I see no reason why the U.S. should not give our own businessmen a break in helping them finance their export credits along the lines of the British and German governments. This is a needed way to compete and to stimulate exports and overseas investments.

COMMODITY PRICES.—We must lend a more sympathetic ear to the Latin-American desire for commodity price stabilization. We must make clear that we are eager to co-operate in finding ways to reduce the hardships of erratic fluctuation. We should examine suggested solutions, commodity by commodity. And we must make up our minds that we are willing to enter into international

---

profits taxes, the concepts which determine whether a tax credit is given frequently make it an inadequate instrument for preventing double taxation. For example, several Latin-American countries impose principal taxes which do not qualify as income taxes under U.S. regulations and therefore cannot be credited against the U.S. tax. The United States has entered into income-tax treaties and conventions with a number of countries around the globe. In Latin America only Honduras has thus far signed such a convention with the United States. Other Latin-American countries have been reluctant to sign such treaties because of their fear that the effect would be to increase U.S. tax revenues at the expense of Latin-American tax revenues.

agreements that will help stabilize markets, even though this seemingly contravenes our basic doctrine of free market prices. We must not seem to be the prime objector to such stabilizing agreements. In some areas and on some commodities we can perhaps be the prime support of them. Such possibilities we should be prepared to examine co-operatively.

LOAN PROGRAMS.—We should provide more credits by stepping up the activities of such institutions as the Inter-American Development bank, the Export-Import bank and the World bank. (To Latin Americans, the United States and its policy are also inextricably identified with the World bank.) The newly established Inter-American Development bank, hastily created in 1959 after Richard Nixon's unhappy experiences in Latin America, should have been started long ago.

In September of 1960 the United States unveiled its major new program to help finance "social improvement" in Latin America. U.S. Undersecretary of State Dillon, at a meeting of finance ministers in Bogotá, disclosed that the United States is prepared to make available an additional $500,000,000 in loans and grants for "social overhead" projects in Latin America in the four fields of housing, land reform, health and education. These are to be of the public type I have been urging, designed to undergird private as well as public economic development.

The Act of Bogotá, signed by the ministers of the United States and of 18 Latin-American nations (Cuba voted "no" and the Dominican Republic was not represented) declared that the "sound social and economic progress of each is of importance to all." This degree of emphasis on social progress as a joint concern is new and important, and so is the emphasis on the basic elements of economic strength.

This new U.S. fund is to be administered mainly through the new Inter-American Development bank. This bank, now set up with an initial capitalization of $1,000,000,000, opened for business October 1, 1960. Whereas the original capitalization of the bank was set up mainly for "hard" loans, repayable in dollars—a policy gravely open to question—the new $500,000,000 will supposedly be earmarked for "soft" loans, repayable in local currency. The then Undersecretary of State Dillon described the $500,000,000 as only the beginning of a great new program.

This is all to the good—though very late. Just as the creation of the Inter-American bank was interpreted widely in Latin America as a reaction to the stoning of Vice-President Nixon—as a sudden awakening by the United States to the depth of the Latin-American problem—the new $500,000,000 is being widely interpreted as a reaction to Castro and to the crisis in U.S.-Cuban relations that developed in the summer of 1960. Indeed, it has already been satirized as the "Castro plan" in Latin America.

Today no adequate organizations exist to whom this new $500,000,000, or further sums to come, can be effectively loaned by the banks. For example, no regional organization devoted to land reform is yet in existence, and only a few countries have national organizations for land reform. Only a few of the 33 resolutions adopted by the finance ministers in Bogotá could be considered as "operations" to be financed through this fund. Almost all of them called for studies, analyses and evaluations, for creations of advisory councils and planning boards. Blueprints for action are now in very short supply in Latin America.

I agree with Senator Smathers that "strict business principles need to be balanced against the social, political and economic dividends which in many cases are more significant than immediate dollar costs." Thus a decisive factor in granting loans can be the need for the project in the over-all economic development of the country involved. This must be weighed along with the questions of repayment. Indeed, I feel that this particular bank should not be run by bankers, with a cold eye fixed primarily on the collateral and the balance sheet, but by men such as Paul Hoffman who ran the Marshall Plan and is now running the Special fund for the UN—men who have the vision and experience to comprehend what is needed for the long pull. This bank's policies should not be "soft-headed" but they should be "soft" in the technical sense that repayment should often be accepted, in part at least, in local currencies, and repayment should often be postponed. This is a policy hard for most professional bankers to swallow.

ECONOMIC PLANNING.—All the lending agencies must learn how better to consult with each other so that they can decide how best to finance the development of Latin America's natural resources. Indeed, they should be closely co-ordinated so that they can better learn to encourage careful preinvestment surveys.

For example former Finance Minister Roberto Vergara of Chile says that his country is 20 years behind in its efforts to study its water resources, and that water geology is almost as important as oil geology. He was certain that Chile could finance its needed electric power plants after such a study had been completed. (I am not so certain!)

For more than ten years the United Nations has carried on at low cost a series of valuable technical assistance programs in Latin America, programs that might well be expanded with further U.S. support. In 1958 and 1959 these UN programs cost only about $13,000,000 a year for 20 countries. Some argue that UN help is more acceptable to Latin-American countries than direct U.S. assistance because it carries no taint of "Yanqui imperialism."

In the past several years the UN's Special Fund under Hoffman has developed an especially promising series of preinvestment surveys for Latin America, financed jointly by the UN and the beneficiary countries. Twenty-four such projects in Latin America have been approved thus far. The first to be completed—at a cost of $250,000—demonstrates the need for and justifies the expenditure of slightly less than $750,000,000 over the next ten years for hydroelectric power development in Argentina. Following the lines of Minister Vergara's suggestion, Chile and the UN Special fund are now co-operating on a survey of Chile's water resources, looking toward an increase of 500,000 hectares of irrigated land and an increase of 1,250,000 kw. of hydroelectric power. Bolivia, Peru and Ecuador are co-operating with the fund on surveys looking toward the opening up of new land for cultivation and settlement.

LABOR.—We should provide help and encouragement to all forces and groups, notably the AFL-CIO, concerned with bolstering free labor unions in Latin America. A dynamic program is needed to offset the Communist campaign of subversion. This is a political objective, but it is also economic. The establishment of active, democratic trade unions is vital to a successful program of industrialization in Latin America. As we found in the Kaiser plant in Argentina, the leadership and incentives provided by some U.S. firms, and channeled in part through the unions, can inspire the best efforts of Latin-American labor. One major goal of U.S. policy should be the strengthening of the free labor movement of Latin America.

MUTUAL ASSISTANCE.—The U.S. needs to seek more dramatic projects for economic co-operation. Much of what the United States has done for the benefit of Latin America has gone relatively unnoticed. Consequently, little good has been achieved in terms of improved understanding of U.S. objectives.

Thus we might help launch a great campaign to eradicate hoof-and-mouth disease among the beef cattle of Latin America. This disease is transmissible to other countries through the meat. President Taylor of the U.S.-owned International Packers, Ltd. estimates that the disease now costs Argentina approximately $150,000,000 a year in foreign exchange, through reduction of exports to the U.S. Now, because of the disease, Germany and Italy are considering following the United States in barring Argentine-killed frozen or cured beef. Pointing to the successful eradication of the disease in northern Mexico, Taylor contends it would be feasible, at a cost of $25,000,000 to $50,000,000, to begin in Patagonia, where the disease is not a problem, and by compulsory vaccination and other methods to push the disease-free area north until the clean zone reached the Argentine Chaco. The same technique could be employed in other affected areas.

This could be a striking example of concrete help from the United States which all Argentinians would understand.[2]

Another dramatic project would be to help clean up the water supply in the big cities of Latin America. The intestinal disorders common to tourists to Mexico City are mockingly known as "Montezuma's revenge." But the last Aztec emperor has now had

[2] After my return to the U.S., I wrote to one of my most knowledgeable acquaintances in Latin America—an American who is himself a potential investor in ranch land—to check further on this suggestion. His answer is so interesting—and so illuminating on the complexities of such a proposal—that I shall quote from it extensively:

"When you talk about a plan to free Latin America from foot and mouth disease you're talking about a few countries in the Southern Cone of South America. Even in these countries you're talking mostly about the low interconnected natural grasslands where cattle movement is intense. (One of the things about FMD [foot-and-mouth disease] that has been learned in very recent years is that on islands or in other isolated areas the disease soon disappears. The cattle get immunized.)

"There are two bad things about FMD: (1) its effect on production, and (2) its effects on markets. The effect on production of FMD, when the disease is widespread and the control measures inadequate, is to decrease production by at least 20%. If this figure is applied to Argentina, which produces over 2 million tons of beef a year, the decrease amounts to more than 400,000 tons, which on the Smithfield market are worth nearly 200 million dollars.

"Uruguay, Brazil and Paraguay—South Cone countries with FMD—have so far shown little concern about the negative effects of the disease on production for domestic consumption. What happens here is that most producers in these countries are absentee owners of big ranches with thousands of cattle. Management decisions regarding the ranch are taken in relation to family needs. And if the family can still go to Paris every year, is there any real reason to get grim about FMD?

"Argentina took this position until a few months ago, when Germany—a country that has brought FMD under control through a massive vaccination campaign—began to complain about outbreaks caused by imports of Argentine beef. Later the Argentine government invited Sir John Hammond, formerly animal physiologist at Cambridge, now England's "Mr. Beef"—the man who constantly tours the world, appraising production in the Commonwealth, Africa and South America, and its effects on future supply to the United Kingdom, to aid in the problem.

"It was Sir John who really galvanized the Argentines into action. 'You must get rid of FMD,' he said to President Frondizi the day after he arrived. 'If you don't, in 10 years—maybe sooner—England will ban your beef just as the U.S. did.' Later he bugged Argentine eyes by talking frankly about the possibility—once free of FMD—of entering the U.S. market, a subject

his revenge and it is time to put an end to it, and to similar troubles all through Latin America, with consequent benefits to the tourist trade.

An attack on infant mortality in rural areas could be organized —the rate is still shockingly high in some districts.

Other projects are doubtless as good or better and may be less costly than these examples. I cover one big and significant opportunity in the following section: the development of Latin America's sadly undernourished universities (and this would not be so costly either). The important suggestion I am advocating here is to find some dramatic and simple and significant idea which can be easily understood by the Latin-American peoples.

At the level of elementary education, I should like to see a plan devised whereby public-school systems in the United States, Canada and western Europe could establish relationships with specific communities in Latin America and through them, as neighbor to neighbor, extend help in the gigantic task of building up their primary-school systems. We have seen such ties established between universities in the United States and those in other parts of the world, and between communities in the "people-

---

that has been giving the Argentines mental hemorrhages ever since 1935 (if memory serves), the year when our Senate failed to ratify a U.S.-Argentine treaty that provided for the import of Argentine meat from Patagonia. Later, about 1941, President Roosevelt, by executive decision, authorized the Secretary of Agriculture to determine whether the U.S. could import from a disease-free part of a country with FMD. The answer was 'yes', and the U.S. imported mutton from Tierra del Fuego for a while—until the U.S. cattle interests got organized and Congress reversed the Secretary's decision.

"I have yet to meet more than an occasional Argentine—no matter how intelligent, well-read, well-traveled, or pro-U.S. he is—who can think unemotionally about the U.S. ban of Argentine meat. For the Argentines this ban is political; they feel the excuses given to justify it merely pretend to be scientific. Even the few Argentines who are unemotional about FMD believe that the U.S. cattle interests will continue to be stronger (as they were in 1941) than any President's or Party's power to promote more trade and better understanding between the two countries. Furthermore, many Argentines feel that freeing their country from FMD would not produce U.S. markets for their meat but would merely produce U.S. tariffs against it.

"In summary the FMD question has caused more bad blood between Argentina and the U.S. than all other questions combined."

to-people" movement. Why could not the same idea now be extended to the elementary schools? This would develop understanding among the children of the hemisphere, as well as help provide financial and other needed material help.

The Improvement of the Universities

When Kenneth Holland, President of the Institute of International Education, was appointed to President Eisenhower's advisory committee on Latin America in the fall of 1959, his first

Credit: John Fell Stevenson

With students of the University of the Andes, Colombia. "Such universities, with more backing, could quickly exercise a powerful influence . . ."

public statement called for a mobilization of private as well as governmental effort to expand education in Latin America.

John D. Rockefeller, Sr. founded the Rockefeller Foundation with the motto, "For the well-being of mankind throughout the world." Of the more than $45,000,000 spent by the Rockefeller foundation in Latin America, a very substantial proportion has been invested in universities, medical schools and other institutions of higher learning.

I know of few ways to contribute to the well-being of mankind that can match the needed development of Latin America's universities. I am persuaded that no single area of action open to the United States and its philanthropists in Latin America is more promising per dollar than the effort to lift the level of its higher education.

An excellent example of our opportunity to help the Latin-American universities help themselves is the present project in the field of economics between the Catholic University in Santiago, Chile, and the University of Chicago. This is financed by Point Four (ICA) funds. In any one year, four members of the Chicago faculty teach in Santiago. Nine of the best Chilean students are now studying for Ph.D.'s in economics at Chicago and all of them have agreed to return to Chile to teach. This exchange seems destined to give Catholic University a distinguished economics faculty. There were 14 such "university-to-university" contracts in operation when Governor Stevenson and I were in Latin America; after we returned to the United States, Columbia University's graduate school of business entered into an arrangement with the University of Buenos Aires business school, but not without protest by a left-wing minority of student representatives on the latter's university council.[3]

An over-all program of investment in the universities of Latin

[3] One observer reported to us that a grave problem in Chile has been posed by the Marxist, left-wing-oriented economists who have come from the university economic departments and who have infiltrated into the Chilean government and economy; we had exactly the same report on the impact of the economics department at the National University of Mexico on the government and attitudes in Mexico. Another close student of Latin America reports that University of Chile economists have been followers of Keynes and Prebisch more than of Marx, and that the Chicago influence at the Catholic University will introduce a third basic viewpoint, that of contemporary "market economics." All these reports show the importance of university training applied to a country's political as well as its economic orientation.

America by the United States government and its agencies, by private industry, by foundations and individuals may sound costly. But the cost is in terms of tens of millions of dollars–and over the next few decades such a program can save the United States billions in terms of economic and other obligations which will otherwise accrue.

Albion Patterson, one of the best-informed and most creative Americans I met in Latin America, who is presently director of U.S. technical co-operation with Argentina at our embassy in Buenos Aires, has proposed that the improvement of Latin-American universities in the strategic fields of science, technology and management should become a major project under Point Four. He suggests that a series of "regional" universities be developed in Latin America, each of which would seek to develop distinction in at least one of the major fields. Galo Plaza of Ecuador advanced to me a proposal somewhat similar. Patterson is also a vigorous proponent of the "Argentine proposal," which has been approved in principle by the Organization of American States. This calls for establishment of regional centers of advanced study and research at key Latin-American universities in six strategic fields: economics, agricultural technology, engineering, business administration, industrial engineering and public administration. The latter three subjects are not now taught in Latin-American universities.

As an example of the deficiencies in a critical field, there is nowhere in Latin America a graduate school of agriculture which combines the teaching, the basic and applied research and the energetic extension activities which might help Latin America achieve its great potential in agriculture. In 1957 there were only 153 agriculturists in the whole of Latin America with a degree of master of science and only 29 with doctorates of philosophy. There are no courses in animal husbandry, as we know this subject, in any Argentine university. Indeed, one of the central problems of higher education in Latin America is that the universities have traditionally existed to train young men for the honorific professions of medicine, law and government. The

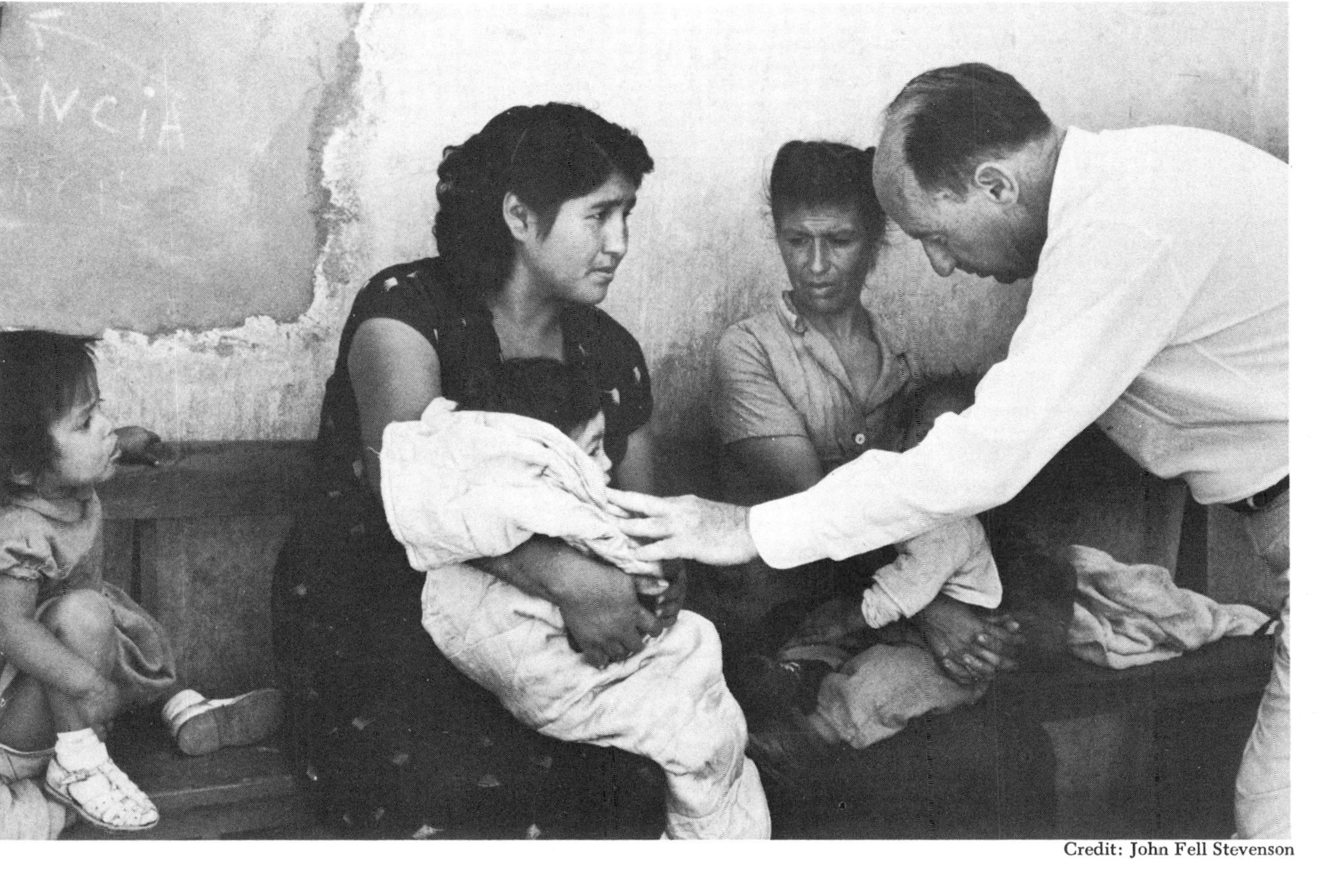

Credit: John Fell Stevenson

Mothers and children in the slums of Lima, Peru. "Average life expectancy is still only 45 years . . ."

figures I have cited for the University of Buenos Aires show that in 1958 a total of 44% of its students were enrolled in the faculties of medicine and law, with another 16% in accounting. Only 12% were enrolled in engineering, 3% in exact sciences and 2% in agronomic sciences. Such proportions do not reflect either national needs or the future opportunities for graduates.

A proposal that I believe has great merit calls for a group of U.S. foundations to concentrate on an attempt to help a single Latin-American university reach such a peak of distinction that it will serve as an example for all other Latin universities. This was the theory on which Johns Hopkins was founded and on which John D. Rockefeller founded the University of Chicago.

Harold Benjamin of the U.S. office of education, consultant to the council on higher education in the American republics, with headquarters in Rio de Janeiro, believes that the decision to create such an institution might have dramatic consequences. He writes me: "A private university under a truly disinterested, non-political board, administered by a rector appointed by the board, and staffed by full-time deans and teachers appointed by the board on recommendation of the rector,[4] could very quickly exercise powerful influence over the whole course of higher education in these countries. Such a university, like the University of California and the University of Wales, could and should have its faculties and institutes in various locales. It could, for example, have its institute of tropical medicine here in Brazil with the Oswaldo Cruz Institute. Its faculty of tropical agriculture could be in Costa Rica, where we now have the Inter-American Institute of Agricultural Sciences. It would have marine biological stations, anthropological institutes, and meteorological departments where they could profit most from the environment. There would have to be a main seat of the university, however, where general education in the sciences, social studies, arts and humanities could be carried on effectively. With its international faculty and student body this university could quickly become a powerful force for a more prosperous and wiser Latin America."

[4] This is the structure of university organization prevalent in the U.S.

THE TRAINING OF STUDENTS ABROAD.—I am sure both Patterson and Benjamin would agree that Latin America's basic problems in higher education must largely be solved within Latin America itself. It cannot be resolved merely by continuing to send students abroad. Nevertheless, for a long time to come far more Latin-American students should be taught English and brought to the U.S. for advanced study. In increasing numbers they should also be sent to Europe. Such training now serves most quickly to introduce modern methods and scholarship to Latin America, as well as to develop cultural relations and friendship in the western world.

At present there are about 8,000 Latin-American students in U.S. colleges and universities. I wish we might aim to add another 2,000 each year for the next four years—to double the number in the next college generation. Indeed, 8,000 more per year would be justified—to step up the number in arithmetical ratio. (The Democratic Advisory council proposes that ways be found to bring to the United States 500,000 students from underdeveloped nations including Latin America!) Although a similar movement of U.S. students to Latin-American universities would help develop mutual understanding in the hemisphere, unhappily until Latin educational standards are improved this is not in the best interests of U.S. students except in Latin-American archaeology or other specialized Latin areas.

When I ask that Latin-American students be taught English so that they can be brought to the U.S. for advanced study, I am touching on a sensitive point. Latin-American students who have come to the United States have not earned a high reputation for scholarship as a group, partly because of language difficulties and partly because of inferior prior instruction as compared with other foreign students. This lack of adequate preparation presents problems in the selection and adjustment of these students.

The head of our student-exchange program in Lima told me that the brightest young men in the University of San Marcos—the oldest university in the hemisphere—often fail to get into U.S. colleges and universities, even when scholarships are available to them, because they cannot pass the required English entrance examination. Yet they may have been studying English for years —with inadequate instructors and techniques. Thus, too high a proportion of the students who are admitted to United States colleges and universities come from the rich homes which can afford private school training in English.

Why would it not be practical for the president of the United States to ask 50,000 or 100,000 U.S. families to take English-speaking Latin-American students into their homes for a year? Certainly each student should be carefully checked for his character and background. Such a massive step would not only be a great propaganda offensive but it would offer a great new channel of understanding on both sides, and it would cost relatively little.

The central and pivotal key to Latin America's future is the education and training of tomorrow's leaders. If we want to help Latin America, we should put more stress upon this and bring more imagination to bear on how to achieve it. A broadly conceived program should be launched with minimum delay.

Further Suggestions in the Cultural and Information Areas

I was most favorably impressed with the staffs of the United States Information Agency (USIA) offices in Latin America. However, the USIA needs bigger budgets, improved personnel, a higher status with the official state department hierarchy and a far more vigorous program. Too much of its present policy is carried on merely to be inoffensive to—or even to impress our own congress—and not enough to reach and impress the people of Latin America. This, however, is not the fault of the men in the field. Broadcasts in Spanish and Portuguese should be greatly stepped up in quantity and improved in quality.

In Washington the USIA should be reintegrated into the State Department, and merged with the cultural affairs area from which it should never have been separated. (The separation was one of Secretary Dulles' less well publicized mistakes, and he was personally and wholly responsible for it.) Its head should be an undersecretary of state, with a voice in the formulation of policy, not merely in its execution. The State Department needs the counsel of its information officers, as the latter need guidance from the political desks.

We were told by the leader of the People's Radical party (the leading opposition party) in Buenos Aires, Crisólogo Larralde, that one of the most important steps the United States could take in Latin America would be to provide factual information about Communism, frankly from our point of view. "Even in papers like *La Nación*," he said, "there is no serious discussion of what's wrong with Communism; very few people here in the Argentine have any idea what's going on behind the 'iron curtain.' They read mostly about Soviet achievements and little else." He went on to say that we should provide more information, too, about the great cultural tradition of the United States, to counteract the impression that the United States is wholly materialistic. I believe he is entirely right, even though the end he seeks is more likely to be achieved in the long run by steady presentation of balanced information than by continual sparring in what Larralde called the "fight of ideas."

The most interesting and presently hopeful phenomena we encountered in this field are the so-called "binational centers." These are the U.S. cultural centers—there are 13 in Chile alone which enroll 7,000 students studying English—carried on under the direction of joint boards of U.S. residents and prominent local citizens, and with the help of officials of the U.S. government and the government of the host country. Because they earn income by teaching English to the tens of thousands who are glad to pay tuition, they require only small subsidies from USIA. In addition to language instruction the centers maintain libraries and conduct programs of lectures, films, concerts, exhibitions and discussions—all designed to further binational understanding. This they do. They will encourage the people of Latin America to visit the U.S. on an ever-increasing scale.

A program to provide better teaching of English in the schools of Latin America can be extremely important for the long range. Our USIA representative in Quito told me that he has assembled ten different courses on how to teach English—from both the United States and Great Britain—and not one is sufficiently simple and elementary for use in the Ecuadorian primary schools. Last year he worked with Ecuador's minister of education to make the teaching of English compulsory—starting with the fourth grade—and now he is embarrassed because he does not have the proper materials to follow through.

Cheaper U.S. books should be made available in great quantities, particularly textbooks. A major translation program should be launched, and I am told a modest start has been made, using funds available under public law 480. I was told that U.S. textbooks cost anywhere from $4.50 to $15 in Ecuador, and that these same books could be printed in Mexico City or Buenos Aires and sold in quantity at 60 cents. (This latter figure is for printing only—and with paper binding—but it seems likely that a "publishing cost" of one third or less of the present prices might be readily achieved.) I would like to hope that the U.S. book-publishing industry, if it were given leadership by the state department or USIA and if it were told that this is a matter of important U.S. policy, might work out such objectives in co-operation with the Latin-American publishing industry.

Language-Study Programs

We can encourage the teaching of Spanish in our schools—as we encourage the study of English below the Rio Grande. The opportunities for Americans to use Spanish will be far greater in the next 50 years than they have ever been. (Spanish is already compulsory in the Miami schools.) Since Portuguese is the language spoken by more than a third of the people in Latin America we should encourage the teaching of this language too. The teaching of the two languages would automatically stimulate greater interest by us in the Latin-American countries. Even if we cannot immediately greatly expand interest in these languages, the effort to do so would be widely heralded by our neighbors in the south. Further, such an effort should stimulate travel to the south. Yes, we should visit them just as we wish them to visit us. Fellowships and grants sponsored by governments, foundations and industry to enable newsmen to visit Latin America on a continuing basis would be of help. If the men are there, they will write the stories.

Philanthropic Efforts

The great private philanthropic institutions of the United States, as Kenneth Holland suggested, should be urged to widen and deepen their interests in Latin America, and not only in the area of higher education. (I applaud the Rockefeller Foundation for the fact that it has maintained programs in Latin America for 30 years.) In Venezuela, for example, we were told by Señora Pérez, President Betancourt's only daughter, that she and her husband are trying to undertake a study of "the image of the American to the Venezuelan and the image of the Venezuelan to the American." A brilliant and attractive girl who studied with her husband at the University of Chicago, Señora Pérez told us that there is no source in all of Venezuela for private funds, even in the tiny amount required for such a modest study. Latin America offers countless projects in the cultural fields made to order for our private foundations.

Expansion by our U.S. philanthropic organizations of their programs in Latin America might have the highly desirable effect of encouraging rich Latin Americans to begin some philanthropic activity of their own. The rich families of Latin America are numerous and some are very rich indeed—but as I have reported we could find no trace of a tradition of private philanthropy. "There are no philanthropists here," said Luis Alberto Sánchez flatly in Lima. This of course is one reason why there are no great private universities in Latin America. It is one reason why Latin Americans look in wonder at the proliferation of philanthropic foundations in the United States.

I believe Governor Stevenson startled some in his audience when he received an honorary degree at the National University of Bogotá. He said, "Businessmen are economic servants for their people. When capital is built it must not be locked up, or spent in luxury for a few, but must be devoted to the further development of the country."

Our foundations set up by our rich men now have an unexcelled opportunity in Latin America. Their leadership is desperately needed, and their example is also.

Credit: John Fell Stevenson

Food market in Santiago, Chile. ". . . irrigated land in the most valuable areas (of Chile) is lying fallow . . ."

In this section, dealing with some possible developments in U.S. policy in relation to Latin America, I have only begun to explore the possibilities of the new U.S. policy which is so urgently needed. I urge my readers to visit Latin America and see for themselves. Then send their suggestions and ideas on policy to their congressmen and senators and to the state department. In Latin America, there is rich opportunity for people-to-people diplomacy, and I realize from my own background as Assistant Secretary of State and U.S. Senator that our future U.S. policy in relation to Latin America, as with all our key policies, can be best hammered out by our leaders on the anvil of U.S. public opinion.

6

And in Concluding—
An Emotional Note

Sixty years ago, in 1900, the Uruguayan philosopher and writer José Enrique Rodó brought out his famous book, *Ariel*, which ever since has inspired the youth of all Latin America. To Rodó, Latin America's role is to play Ariel to the Caliban of the United States.

It is important for us in the United States better to understand that Latin America's very real admiration for the United States—"our mania for the north," in Rodó's phrase—is a qualified admiration. The qualification springs not so much from envy but from the belief that the moral and intellectual outlook of Latin America represents a distillation of Mediterranean culture with which the United States has not been equally blessed.

Of the United States, Rodó wrote:

> Its prosperity is as immense as its incapability of satisfying even a mediocre view of human destiny. Titanic in its concentration of human will-power, with unprecedented triumphs in all spheres of material aggrandizement, its civilization yet produces as a whole a singular impression of insufficiency, of emptiness.
>
> As fast as the utilization genius of that nation takes on a more

> defined character, franker, narrower yet, with the intoxication of material prosperity, so increases the impatience of its sons to spread it abroad by propaganda, and think it predestined for a Roman role.

Thus Latin Americans feel they have something to teach us—and they have.

I would like to urge that all of us in the United States, from the State Department to the man in the street, reappraise some of the outworn illusions we tend to cherish about Latin America and its people. We must attune our ears to the voices that are raised in both impassioned clamor and quiet criticism. Somehow we have gone astray since the days of the good neighbor policy when we and they were moving forward, together, as partners in the Americas.

We must remember that we are dealing with youth. Their leaders, the prime movers of the new Latin America, are young in years. Further, these are young nations, only recently born into an industrial world. And youth is impatient, full of hopes and ideals that are not always possible of realization. But, as Governor Stevenson, said to a group of students, "If this is so, I hope it will always be so, for the idealism of today is the hope for the practice of tomorrow."

We must not expect the Latin Americans to act as we do, or think as we think. We must have patience and must understand that their first halting steps toward social democracy start from a base very different from our own. And we must understand their pride in their own values and their faith that they can contribute to the cultural welfare of the world.

Above all, we must recapture the glow of the friendship which we once enjoyed together. We must remind ourselves that we must be concerned about Latin America not because it is the strategic thing to do or because there are more and noisier Communists south of us than there used to be. We must be concerned because we really want to be good neighbors. Our leaders must see to it that our people understand that these are not strangers, but neighbors. And the neighbors must be made to know that we agree with them that our fate and future is bound up inextricably with theirs.

For better or for worse the United States must face the responsibility of leadership in the hemisphere. We have the money, the know-how, the military power, the technology, the prestige and the democratic traditions that Latin-American countries largely lack. The first goal of this leadership must be to win trust and friendship, to set an example that will cause the youth of Latin America to follow us of their own choice. We must think of tomorrow as well as of today. We must continuously demonstrate our respect for their own finest values.

Suggested Readings*

The Voice of Latin America Has Many Accents (Chapter 1)

Alexander, Robert J., *The Bolivian National Revolution* (New Brunswick, Rutgers University Press, 1958). A friendly interpretation of the Bolivian Revolution since 1952.

Davis, Harold E. (ed.), *Government and Politics in Latin America* (New York, The Ronald Press, 1958). Useful articles on political groups and the structure and functions of political power.

Fitzgibbon, Russell H., *Uruguay: Portrait of a Democracy* (New Brunswick, Rutgers University Press, 1954). Friendly examination of Latin America's most democratic republic.

Fluharty, Vernon L., *Dance of the Millions: Military Rule and the Social Revolution in Colombia, 1930–1956* (Pittsburgh, University of Pittsburgh Press, 1957). The best survey in English of a highly important era of Colombian history. Perhaps overly sympathetic to the military dictatorship of Rojas Pinilla.

Freyre, Gilberto, *New World in the Tropics* (New York, Alfred A. Knopf, 1959). A highly nationalistic interpretation of the culture of modern Brazil by that nation's outstanding sociologist.

Hanke, Lewis, *Modern Latin America* (New York, D. Van Nostrand, 1959). In two brief paperback volumes the author traces Latin America's historical evolution, and provides the reader with several

* These references, arranged by subject, are keyed to each chapter. I acknowledge gratefully the help of Professor John J. Johnson of Stanford University in the compiling and annotation of this selective bibliography for readers who will, we both hope, want to expand their knowledge and understanding of Latin America through these readings.—W.B.

excellent selections from the writings of well-known Latin American authorities.

Herring, Hubert, *A History of Latin America* (New York, Alfred A. Knopf, 1961). The most readable general history of Latin America.

Hispanic American Report (Stanford, 1948 —). A monthly round up of developments in Spain, Portugal, and Latin America.

International Bank for Reconstruction and Development, *The Economic Development of Venezuela* (Baltimore, The Johns Hopkins Press, 1961). Up-to-date. Data organized in readily usable form.

Karnes, Thomas L., *The Failure of Union: Central America, 1824–1960* (Chapel Hill, the University of North Carolina Press, 1961). Provides a sound survey of an important and often neglected area.

Martz, John D., *Central America: the Crisis and the Challenge* (Chapel Hill, the University of North Carolina Press, 1959). Useful descriptive survey of the several republics of Central America.

Pike, Frederick B. (ed.), *Freedom and Reform in Latin America* (Notre Dame, University of Notre Dame Press, 1959). Twelve article-chapters by recognized authorities that deal with freedom and reform in Latin America during the last half century.

Scott, Robert E., *Mexican Government in Transition* (Urbana, University of Illinois Press, 1959). Unquestionably the best study on Mexico in nearly a decade.

Szulc, Tad, *Twilight of the Tyrants* (New York, Henry Holt and Company, 1959). Biographic sketches of five major military dictators of Latin America during the 1950s by a highly competent journalist and astute observer.

Whitaker, Arthur P., *The United States and Argentina* (Cambridge, Harvard University Press, 1954). Somewhat dated since the fall of Perón but still the best general study in English on Argentina.

The Struggle Upward Towards the Sun (Chapter 2)

Inter-American Economic Affairs (Washington, 1947 —). A quarterly concerned mainly with the economic problems of Latin America, including the economics of U.S. aid to Latin America.

The National Planning Association's series, *United States Business Performance Abroad*, contains four studies on Latin America; R. Wood, "Sears Roebuck de México," (Washington, 1953); E. W. Burgess, "Casa Grace in Peru," (1954); W. C. Taylor, "The Creole Petroleum Corporation in Venezuela," (1955); and S. May and Galo Plaza, "The United Fruit Company in Latin America," (1958).

Poblete Troncoso, Moisés and Burnett, Ben G., *The Rise of the Latin American Labor Movement* (New Haven, Bookman Associates, 1960). Traces the development of the labor movement in each of the republics of Latin America, with special attention to the movements in Argentina and Chile.

Teichert, Pedro C. M., *Economic Policy Revolution and Industrialization in Latin America* (University, Mississippi, University of Mississippi, Bureau of Business Research, 1959). Broad coverage with strong emphasis on recent developments.

United Nations, Economic Commission for Latin America, *Economic Survey of Latin America* (Lake Success, 1948 ––). This annual is an invaluable source on economic problems and trends in Latin America.

The Threatening Cloud—Communism and Castroism (Chapter 3)

Alexander, Robert J., *Communism in Latin America* (New Brunswick, Rutgers University Press, 1957). A wealth of factual information.

Allen, Robert L., *Soviet Influence in Latin America: the Role of Economic Relations* (Washington, Public Affairs Press, 1959). Useful discussion of Soviet-bloc-Latin American trade and commercial policies, Latin America's motives and goals, and Soviet-bloc capabilities.

American Universities Field Staff, *Report Service* (American Universities Field Staff, Inc., 1952 ––). These reports are concisely written statements ordinarily on quite specific subjects. During 1960 Irving P. Pflaum did twelve reports on Cuba. The reports by Richard W. Patch on Peru and Bolivia and by Kalman Silvert on Chile and Argentina are, in general, outstandingly good.

Current History (April, 1961) contains articles on contemporary Brazil, Argentina, Central America, Cuba, Peru and Venezuela and Latin America in world affairs.

Draper, Theodore, "Castro's Cuba," *New Leader*, March 27, 1961. Discusses the reorientation of the Castro revolution and examines critically some of the pro-Castro literature that has appeared in English.

Johnson, John J., *Political Change in Latin America: The Emergence of the Middle Sectors* (Stanford, Stanford University Press, 1958). A study of the political groups in Latin America whose dominance is now being challenged by the Castroites and Communists.

"Latin America's Nationalistic Revolutions," comprising fifteen timely articles on contemporary Latin America, mostly by responsible academicians, appeared as the March, 1961 issue of *The Annals of the American Academy of Political and Social Science.*

Lieuwin, Edwin, *Arms and Politics in Latin America* (New York, Frederick A. Praeger, Inc., 1960). An excellent exploratory study with a strong emphasis upon the implication of U.S. military aid to Latin America and U.S. support of military dictators.

Philips, R. Hart, *Cuba: Island of Paradox* (New York, McDowell, Obolensky, 1959). One of the more objective of the many studies on Cuba since the coming to power of Fidel Castro.

Schneider, Ronald M., *Communism in Guatemala: 1944–1954* (New York, Frederick A. Praeger, 1959). A mine of information about Guatemala and the Communist techniques.

Education—The Key to Latin America's Future (Chapter 4)

Bonilla, Frank, "The Student Federation of Chile: 50 Years of Political Action," *Journal of Inter-American Studies* (July, 1960). A thoughtful examination of a highly important subject.

Dale, George Allan, *Education in the Republic of Haiti* (Washington, U.S. Dept. of Health, Education, and Welfare, 1959). Objective Survey.

"Education and Social Change in Latin America," *Rural Sociology* (March, 1960). The entire issue is devoted to Latin America and provides a scholarly evaluation of the problems of rural education and urbanization.

Faust, Augustus P., *Brazil: Education in an Expanding Economy* (Washington, U.S. Dept. of Health, Education, and Welfare, 1959).

Johnston, Marjorie C. *Education in Mexico* (Washington, U.S. Dept. of Health, Education, and Welfare, 1956). A comprehensive presentation with emphasis on public elementary and secondary education.

Río, Ángel del (ed.), *Responsible Freedom in the Americas* (New York, Doubleday, 1955). A useful compendium of current thought on the school in Latin American society.

Samper, Armando, *A Case Study of Cooperation in Secondary Education in Chile* (Washington, National Planning Association, 1957). A study in technical cooperation.

How Can the United States Best Help Latin America Help Itself (Chapter 5)

The American Assembly, *The United States and Latin America* (n.p., 1959). Written to increase public understanding of Latin America.

A generally friendly point of view towards the area is taken by the six contributors.

Dozer, Donald M., *Are We Good Neighbors?* (Gainesville, University of Florida Press, 1959). The answer is a rather emphatic no.

Houston, John, *Latin America in the United Nations* (New York, Carnegie Endowment for International Peace, 1956). Good coverage.

Perkins, Dexter, *The United States and Latin America* (Baton Rouge, Louisiana State University Press, 1961). An old pro takes a quick look at Latin America in terms of national security, political relations, and economic relations.

Social Change in Latin America Today (New York, Harper and Brothers, 1960). Six social anthropologists look at the "historyless" people of Latin America and what they mean in terms of future U.S.-Latin American relations.

United States Senate, *United States-Latin American Relations* (Washington, Govt. Printing Office, 1960). Seven worthwhile studies done by the staffs of universities and research institutes for the Subcommittee on American Republics Affairs of the Committee on Foreign Relations, United States Senate.

INDEX